The Zbaraz Memorial Book
(Zbarazh, Ukraine)

Translation of
Sefer Zbaraz

Original Yizkor Book Editor: Moshe Sommerstein

Published in Tel Aviv 1983

Published by JewishGen

An Affiliate of the Museum of Jewish Heritage—A Living Memorial to the Holocaust
New York

Zbaraz Yizkor Book

Zbaraz: the Zbaraz Memorial Book (Zbarazh, Ukraine)
Translation of: *Sefer Zbaraz*
  Edited by Moshe Sommerstein,
  Published in Tel Aviv 1983 by The Organization of Former Zbaraz Residents
  Originally in Hebrew, Yiddish and English, 128 pages

Translations by Yaacov David Shulman (unless otherwise noted)
Layout: Donni Magid
Cover Design: Nina Schwartz, Impulse Graphics LLC

Published by JewishGen, Inc.
An Affiliate of the Museum of Jewish Heritage
A Living Memorial to the Holocaust
36 Battery Place, New York, NY 10280

JewishGen, Inc. is not responsible for inaccuracies or omissions in the original work and makes no representations regarding the accuracy of this translation. Digital images of the original book's contents can be seen online at the New York Public Library website.

The mission of the JewishGen organization is to produce a translation of the original work, and we cannot verify the accuracy of statements or alter facts cited.

Printed in the United States of America by Lightning Source, Inc.

Library of Congress Control Number (LCCN): 2018965012
ISBN: 978-1-939561-72-5 (hard cover: 172 pages, alk. paper)

JewishGen and the Yizkor Books in Print Project

This book has been published by the **Yizkor Books in Print Project**, as part of the **Yizkor Book Project** of JewishGen, Inc.

JewishGen, Inc. is a non-profit organization founded in 1987 as a resource for Jewish genealogy. Its website [www.jewishgen.org] serves as an international clearinghouse and resource center to assist individuals who are researching the history of their Jewish families and the places where they lived. JewishGen provides databases, facilitates discussion groups, and coordinates projects relating to Jewish genealogy and the history of the Jewish people. In 2003, JewishGen became an affiliate of the **Museum of Jewish Heritage—A Living Memorial to the Holocaust** in New York.

The **JewishGen Yizkor Book Project** was organized to make more widely known the existence of Yizkor (Memorial) Books written by survivors and former residents of various Jewish communities throughout the world. Later, volunteers connected to the different destroyed communities began cooperating to have these books translated from the original language—usually Hebrew or Yiddish—into English, thus enabling a wider audience to have access to the valuable information contained within them. As each chapter of these books was translated, it was posted on the JewishGen website and made available to the general public.

The **Yizkor Books in Print Project** began in 2011 as an initiative to print and publish Yizkor Books that had been fully translated, so that hard copies would be available for purchase by the descendants of these communities and also by scholars, universities, synagogues, libraries, and museums.

These Yizkor books have been produced almost entirely through the volunteer effort of researchers from around the world, assisted by donations from private individuals. The books are printed and sold at near cost, so as to make them as affordable as possible. Our goal is to make this important genre of Jewish literature and history available in English in book form, so that people can have the personal histories of their ancestral towns on their bookshelves for themselves and for their children and grandchildren.

A list of all published translated Yizkor Books in the project with prices and ordering information can be found at:
http://www.jewishgen.org/Yizkor/ybip.html

Lance Ackerfeld, Yizkor Book Project Manager
Joel Alpert, Yizkor-Book-in-Print Project Coordinator

JewishGen
Yizkor Book Project

This book is presented by the
Yizkor Books in Print Project
Project Coordinator: Joel Alpert

Part of the
Yizkor Books Project of JewishGen, Inc.
Project Manager: Lance Ackerfeld

These books have been produced solely through volunteer effort
of individuals from around the world. The books are printed and
sold at near cost, so as to make them as affordable as possible.

Our goal is to make this history and important genre of Jewish
literature available in English in book form so that people can have
the near-personal histories of their ancestral towns on their bookshelves for themselves and for their children and grandchildren.

Any donations to the Yizkor Books Project are appreciated.

Please send donations to:
Yizkor Book Project
JewishGen
36 Battery Place
New York, NY 10280

JewishGen, Inc. is an affiliate of the
Museum of Jewish Heritage
A Living Memorial to the Holocaust

Acknowledgments

Many thanks to the translator Yaacov David Shulman, who did translated most of the book.

Our sincere appreciation to Helen Rosenstein Wolf
for typing up the English text to facilitate its addition to the Yizkor Book Project.

Special thanks to the National Yiddish Book Center in Amherst, Massachusetts and the New York Public Library for supplying the high resolution images used in this book.

———

Notes to the Reader:

We apologize ahead of time for the poor quality of images in the book. Often these images had been scanned from the original Yizkor books which were of poor quality to begin with, being copies of old photographs. Each transfer results in loss of quality. We have done the best we could, given the original material and the resources and technology at hand. Even though images often appear of higher quality on computer screens, that does not transfer to high quality images in print. A reader can view the original scans on the web sites listed below.

Within the text the reader will note "{34}" standing ahead of a paragraph. This indicates that the material translated below was on page 34 of the original book. However, when a paragraph was split between two pages in the original book, the marker is placed in this book after the end of the paragraph for ease of reading.

Also please note that all references within the text of the book to page numbers, refer to the page numbers of the original Yizkor Book.

The original book can be seen online at the New York Public Library site:
http://yizkor.nypl.org/index.php?id=2099
or at the Yiddish Book Center web site:
https://www.yiddishbookcenter.org/search/collection/%22NYPL-Yiddish%2520Book%2520Center%2520Yizkor%2520Book%2520Collection%22

https://digitalcollections.nypl.org/collections/yizkor-book-collection?id=1178#/?tab=navigation

In order to obtain a list of all Shoah victims from Zbaraz, the reader should access the Yad Vashem web site listed below; one can also search for specific family names using family name option. These lists are continually updated by Yad Vashem, so it is worthwhile to periodically search these lists.

There is much valuable information available on this web site, including the Pages of Testimony, etc.
http://yvng.yadvashem.org

A list of this book and all books available in the Yizkor-Book-In-Print Project along with prices is available at:
http://www.jewishgen.org/Yizkor/ybip.html

Geopolitical Information:

Located at 49°40' Latitude and 25°47' Longitude
12 miles NE of Ternopil

Alternate names for the town are: Alternate names: Zbarazh [Ukr, Rus, Yid], Zbaraż [Pol], Sbarasch [Ger], Sparach, Zbarezh

Period	Town	District	Province	Country
Before WWI (c. 1900):	Zbaraż	Zbaraż	Galicia	Austrian Empire
Between the wars (c. 1930):	Zbaraż	Zbaraż	Tarnopol	Poland
After WWII (c. 1950):	Zbarazh			Soviet Union
Today (c. 2000):	Zbarazh			Ukraine

Note: Jewish Population in 1890: 3,631
Ukrainian/Russian: Збараж. Yiddish: זבאראזש. Hebrew: זברז'

Nearby Jewish Communities:
      Stryyivka 5 miles SSE
      Vyshhorodok 11 miles NE
      Ternopil 12 miles SW
      Kam'yanky 13 miles SE
      Vishnevets 16 miles N
      Novyy Oleksinets 17 miles NW
      Skalat 18 miles SSE
      Pidvolochys'k 19 miles ESE
      Belozërka 19 miles ENE

MAP OF UKRAINE IN 2014

Hebrew Title Page of Original Yiddish or Hebrew Book

זכור את אשר עשה לך עמלק!   לזכור ולא לשכוח!

נר נשמה לקדושי זברז' והסביבה והנצחת עולם לשמם ולדמותם
מאת שרידיהם בישראל ובתפוצות.

א נשמה — ליכט פאר די זבארז'ער קדושים און א אייביקער
אנדענק פאר זייערע נעמן און געשטאלטן, — פון זייערע לעבן
געבליבענע אין ישראל און אין דער נארער יידישער וועלט.

Translation of the Title Page of Original Yiddish Book

THE ZBARAZ MEMORIAL BOOK

REMEMBER WHAT AMALEK DID TO YOU !
TO REMEMBER AND NOT TO FORGET !

An everlasting memorial to the sacred memory of the martyrs
of Zbaraz, dedicated by their descendants in Israel
and the Diaspora.

Zbaraz Yizkor Book

Cover Photo Credits:

Synagogue, 1916, and *Jews on the Street, 1916:* Courtesy of August Thiry. Photos taken by Belgians of the armored car unit ACM in early 1916.

Ruined Jewish Houses and *Ruined Jewish House:* Photos ©2007 by Alex Denysenko, Living Family Genealogy and Historical Family Research, http://ukrainelivingfamily.blogspot.com.

Alex Denysenko graduated from Lviv State University, and studied at Institute of International Tourism in Moscow, Russia; and Yad Vashem International School of Holocaust Studies, Jerusalem, Israel. Since 1991, he has worked as a researcher and guide in research/teaching/touring programs. These projects deal with the Jewish segment of Central European history to find documentation/material/oral evidence about Jewish residents and their heritage.

Alex has also conducted applied research projects about Jewish-Polish-Ukrainian-Russian-German relations in Galicia connected with the events of the First and Second World Wars, as well as border changes/resettlements/genocide that resulted from the above conflicts.

Postcard, Zbaráz Main Square, 1917: Photo by P. Grünberg. Source: National Library of Poland via Polona.pl. Public domain.

Postcard of Zbaráz: Pond from the side of Bazarzyniec. Photo by Nakł. J. Dubiner, 1927-1936. Source: National Library of Poland via Polona.pl. Public domain.

Table of Contents

Family Notes

[Page 4]

May the Nation of Israel Remember
[Memorial prayer]

יזכור עם ישראל

ברטט נפש, בחרדת לב וביראת כבוד את הנשמות הטהורות
והזכות של בניו ובנותיו אשר הושמדו בכל מיני מיתות
משונות, מי בחנק ובמשרפות, מי בתאי הגזים בבלזיק, מי
בגרושים ובמחנות עבודה על אדמת נכר דווית דם ודמע,
בכל מקומות ההרג והטבח, שנתקדישו בקדושה עניויים.

נזכור את אבותינו ואמהותינו, אחינו ואחיותינו, ילדינו
ונכדינו וכל יתר היקרים שנשחטו, נשרפו ונחנקו על לא עוון
בכפם, רק באשר יהודים המה, צאצאי נביאי ישראל השואף
לדרור, צדק ושלום.

נזכור את נשמת הגבורים אשר השליכו את עצמם
מנגד, טרפו חייהם בכפם ויחרפו נפשם על קדוש השם ועל
כבוד האדם והוציאו את נשמתם עם קריאת נצח ,,שמע
ישראל" ו,,התקוה" על שפתותיהם.

נזכור אנו מתוך הרגשת שכול ויתמות את הקהילה
הקדושה והיקרה זברז' והסביבה.

אנו מתאבלים ומבכים את העיירה היקרה, השדודה,
השוממה והעזובה מאין עדה ויושב יהודי בהן.

לא נשכח קדושי זברז' והסביבה וזכר חסד נעוריך
לא ימוש מלבנו לעולם.

ת. נ. צ. ב. ה.

With a trembling soul, with a shuddering heart and with the greatest respect for the pure and pristine souls of our sons and daughters who were destroyed by every means of violent murder: by strangulation and by fire, by the gas chambers in Belzets, driven away to work camps upon foreign land soaked with blood and tears, on killing and slaughter sites sanctified by their torment.

We recall our fathers and mothers, our brothers and sisters, our children and grandchildren, and all of the other precious ones who were slaughtered, burned and strangled for one reason only: because they were Jews, the descendants of the prophets of Israel, a nation that yearns for freedom, justice and peace.

We recall the souls of the valiant ones who cast aside their lives, put their lives in their hands and sacrificed themselves for the sanctification of God and the honor of man, who gave up their lives with the eternal proclamation of "Hear O Israel" and with Hatikvah on their lips.

We recall with feelings of bereavement, as orphans, the holy and precious community of Zbarazh and its environs.

We mourn and weep over the precious town, plundered, desolate and abandoned, without any Jewish community and inhabitants.

We will not forget the martyrs of Zbarazh and its environs. The memory of the kindness of your youth will never leave our hearts.

May their souls be bound in the knot of life.

[Page 5]

"God, Filled with Compassion"
[Prayer for the Soul of the Departed]

אל מלא רחמים

בורא ארץ ומרומים, שומע שועת עגומים, דיין אלמנות
ויתומים, אל נא תחשה לדם עמך ישראל השפוך כמים, המצא
מנוחה נכונה על כנפי השכינה, במעלות קדושים וטהורים כזהר
הרקיע מזהירים, את נשמותיהם של שש מאות רבבות אלפי
ישראל, ובתוכם בני קהילתנו הקדושה זבר׳ והקהילות הקדושות
שבסביבתה, אלפי אנשים ונשים, ילדים וילדות, עוללים וטף,
שנהרגו ושנחנקו ושהוטבעו ושנשרפו ושנקברו חיים בידי
העמלקים הגרמנים, הטמאים והאכזריים. — בגיטאות זבר׳
וסביבתה ובתאי הגזים בבלזץ וביתר מחנות המות של האויב
הנאצי ונוריהם, כולם קדושים וטהורים וביניהם גבורי הרוח,
גאונים וצדיקים, תמימים וישרי לב, רבנים וחסידים, אדירי תורה
ותלמידיהם, רופאים, עורכי־דין, שופטים ובעלי מלאכה, כולם
ידי׳חרוצים. — יזכרם השם לטובה, ובגן־עדן תהא מנוחתם,
בעל הרחמים יסתירם בסתר כנפיו לעולמים ויצרור בצרור החיים
את נשמותיהם, ד׳ הוא נחלתם, והוא ינקום את נקמתם ויזכור
לנו עקדתם ותעמוד לנו ולכל ישראל זכותם, ארץ אל תכסי דמם
ואל יהי מקום לזעקתם, בזכותם ישובו נדחי ישראל לאחוזתם,
וחקדושים האלה תהא לזכרון תמיד לפני השם צדקתם, יבואו
שלום, וינוחו על משכבותם ויקיצו ויעמדו לקץ הימים לחייתם.
ונאמר אמן !

Creator of the earth and the heights, You Who hear the outcry of the disconsolate, Judge of widows and orphans, do not remain silent before the blood of Your nation Israel that is spilled like water. Grant them proper rest upon the wings of God's Presence, on the lofty level of the holy and pure ones, who shine with the brightness of the firmament, the souls of six million Jews, among them the people of our holy community of Zbarazh and the surrounding holy communities, thousands of men and women, boys and girls, babies and infants, who were killed, strangled, drowned, burned and buried alive by the unclean and inhuman Amelekite Germans in the ghettos of Zbarazh and its environs, in the gas chambers in Belzets and in the other death camps of the Nazi enemy and their collaborators–all of the Jews holy and pure, among them heroes of the spirit, prodigies and righteous people, blameless and upright, rabbis and Hasidim, aristocrats of the Torah and their students, doctors, lawyers, judges and craftsmen, all of them diligent–may Hashem remember them for good and may they rest in the Garden of Eden. May the Master of compassion hide them in the concealment of His wings forever and bind their souls in the knot of life, which is their inheritance. May He take vengeance and recall for us their slaughter. May their merit accrue to us and to all Israel. Earth, do not conceal their blood and do not allow their outcry to continue! In their merit, may the outcasts of Israel return to their estate. And may the righteousness of these holy martyrs be a permanent memory before Hashem. May they come to peace and rest, and awaken and stand at the end of days resurrected. And let us say, Amen!

———

[Page 7]

This Book
Moshe Sommerstein

Years ago, a small group of people, émigrés from Zbarazh, had the idea of establishing a memorial for this ancient community, whose generations and influence spread beyond its limited borders. They wanted to commemorate their community, this glorious community, whose Jews were lost in the Holocaust.

It was difficult to attain the historical material needed to give an impression of the city, material that would testify to the cultural life of this community and its inhabitants. We know that this is the last chance to find and save documents and papers. We gathered very little, but we put together stories, descriptions, pictures and memories that will give some idea about our community.

We had to search for all material possible to reconstruct Jewish and Zionist Zbarazh, to find documents that describe the destruction of the city and the extermination of its Jewish residents by Hitler's soldiers, and gather material about the deeds of blood and acts of might as related by the people who personally experienced the terror of those days and who were saved miraculously and who live today in Israel, Europe, the United States, Argentina and Australia.

With the passage of time, people are passing away, and the survivors of Zbarazh and its environs who live in Israel are growing fewer. Our recognition of this fact intensified our feeling of urgency and inspired us to record what people have to tell. If we have succeeded in completing this mission, even if we have gathered little, we have done a great service for ourselves and for our children.

We will tell our youth about our holy community, and that will be a small consolation for us: that we have established a memorial of all of our holy martyrs who were annihilated in the Holocaust, and whom we loved.   **May their memory be blessed.**

[Page 8]

**To: Our brothers and sisters,
compatriots, across the entire world.**

**From: The Central Committee of Zbarazh Jews
in Israel, P.O.B. 22186, Tel Aviv.**

Zbarazh was a town in Galicia (Poland) that was famed as a gathering of Jewish *maskilim*, rabbis, outstanding individuals, writers, Yiddish and Hebrew schools, Torah study halls, Hasidim and forward–facing youth with great national pride–a town whose sons and daughters played a major role in building the land of Israel.

Among the bloody, tragic events of the destruction of the Jewish nation in Poland, so too the Jewish population of our town went upon the "last way" of sanctification of God's name.

Almost an entire generation has lived since that tragic time, but the blood of our precious, tortured parents, brothers, sisters, children, relatives, neighbors and young comrades has not ceased crying out from the graves of the slaughtering fields, Belzets and Majdanek, reminding us to "remember what Amalek did to you" and calling for vengeance against the enemies of Israel, who are still walking free across the entire world, and there is no justice and no judge.

We here in Israel, a large part of the survivors, undertook the holy task and mission of establishing a living monument to the martyrs of our town in the form of a Yizkor book that will reflect the one–time life of our town of Zbarazh.

[Page 9]

We turn to you, beloved sisters and brothers across the entire world, to make the effort to respond properly with an appropriate sum of money so that it will be possible for us to publish this Yizkor book for the fallen martyrs of Zbarazh. May the pages of this book tell about the destruction and downfall of our former community, which lived and flowered, and then suddenly disappeared, murdered by the criminals of the Nazi regime and the bands of their murderous collaborators.

We await your extended hand and assistance to help us realize our dream of many years to honor the names of our holy martyrs by publishing this monument in words and pictures. You are requested to send us materials (if you have such).

P.S. Please send us the addresses of all of our brothers and sisters that you know of, so that we will be able to write to each one individually about the monument that we have decided to publish in Israel. We will send a copy to everyone who participates in granting assistance to this project.

Every donor is requested to send a donation to the following address:

> *Sefer Yizkor* (Organization of Zbarazh Émigrés)
> Account number 489720
> Bank Hapoalim, Haifa, Israel
> Or:
> Mordechai Sherlag
> Rechov Pinsker 11
> Haifa 32715

[Page 10]

Central Committee of the Jews of Zbarazh in Israel, 26 De Haas Street, Tel Aviv

Moshe Sommerstein, President
Mordechai Sherlag, Treasurer

Nachman Karmi, Stella Seidenberg, Gershon Landsberg, Icchok Wechsler, Yesaiahu Rothman, Swadron Moshe, Weihrauch Moshe, Zalman Rosenberg–committee members.

Tel Aviv, Haifa, 23 Adar 5739 (22.3.1979)

———

[Page 11]

Federation of Outgoing Zbaraz and Vicinity

Moshe Sommerstein, Advocate

26, De-Haas Street, Tel Aviv, 62-667, Israel

To:

—————————————

—————————————

—————————————

Dears, Sisters and Brothers,

According to the decision of our last General Assembly, which took place on the 29.6.1980 in Tel Aviv, where there has been elected a Committee to consider organization and publication to perpetuate the memory of the fallen "KDOSHIM" in our town Zbaraz and vicinity, through publishing a Book "ISCOR".

The members of this Committee are from Haifa and Tel Aviv.

Herewith, is the decision:

To apply in writing to all outgoing Zbaraz and vicinity people wherever they are asking to supply us with various material in writing, pictures, photos, personal impressions and any material connected with the holocaust in the years 1939-1945 in order to start work regarding the "ISCOR" Book.

To ask all the Zbaraz people all over the world to prepare personal scripts in Hebrew, Yiddish, English, Polish and German, their personal difficulties in the past and experience in the holocaust, how they were persecuted, suffering and punished.

[Page 12]

To ask all the Zbaraz people to help us financially in publishing this Book "Iscor". Without their help, we cannot make it.

All contributions, donations, please send to the address: "SEFER ISCOR", Irgun Yozei Zbaraz, Bank Hapoalim, Haifa, ISRAEL.

Cordially,
Moshe Sommerstein
Advocate
The President
Mordechai Sherlag
Treasurer

The Members of the Committee

Nachman Karmi, Stella Seidenwerg, Gershon Landsberg, Icchok Wechsler, Yesaiahu Rothman, Swadron Moshe, Weihrauch Moshe, Zalman Rosenberg.

Tel Aviv
23.11.1980

———

[Page 13]

Foreword
Moshe Sommerstein

Very few Jews of the city of Zbarazh and its environs survived the Holocaust. Most of those who survived came to Israel in the years 1955–1960, and they all found work and were integrated into its life.

The Jewish community of Zbarazh numbered about 80,000 people, including Jews who had fled from the Polish territory occupied by the Germans at the beginning of the war. The Jews were liquidated by the Nazis and their collaborators in the town or in other murder sites.

In Israel, the survivors who had been in Zbarazh, newcomers and old–timers, got together. Together, we number a few hundred people.

The Grove of a Thousand Trees in the Forest of the Martyrs.
In memory of the Jews of Zbarazh and its environs.

[Page 14]

[Page 15]

Monument in memory of our children who died in the Holocaust
A gift of Dr. Monya Froynglass (of blessed memory) of Zbarazh, in the Holocaust Cellar in Jerusalem

[Page 16]

Over the years, we wanted to erect a monument in memory of the members of our families who were put to death in many terrible ways–in forests, in the ghetto, in the fields and in bunkers, in gas chambers and in fiery ovens that our enemies set up in order to annihilate us–but we did not have the means to do so. And so for many years we made do with memorial gatherings for our martyrs in Haifa and in Tel Aviv, where most of our people live. And we do that to this day.

In the years 1959–1960, we bought a grove of a thousand trees in the Forest of the Martyrs, where we gather next to the monument and recall the victims of our city. This year as well we organized such a gathering on Holocaust Memorial Day.

In addition, two small monuments were erected on Mt. Zion in Jerusalem, and a monument in memory of our murdered children was built in the Holocaust Cellar. This monument was set up with the financial assistance of Dr. Monya Froynglass (of blessed memory) of Zbarazh. But we could not manage to publish a Yizkor book because we lacked the means to do so.

We turned both personally and officially to the organization of the Jews of Zbarazh in the United States and to its president, Isolde Shpeizer, who promised to help us, and we received word by telephone that they decided to send us $1800. For this help we thank them–in particular, we thank the new president, Lester Shpeizer, and the organization's secretary, Peninah Veit.

We hope that we will complete this project, now that the émigrés of Zbarazh who live in Vienna, Mr. Carl Kahane, Joseph Gutfrei of Toronto and others have helped us with significant sums. This time we will overcome the difficulties and, with the aid of our compatriots in Israel, we will establish a memorial for our community in the form of this book.

This Yizkor book, which will be distributed to the émigrés of Zbarazh in Israel and across the world, will bring the story of this small community to the broader public. The community of Zbarazh played an important role in the history of the Jews of Poland. This community achieved much in the fields of culture and education; its inhabitants performed mighty deeds before the war and during the years of the Holocaust.

[Page 17]

May we be worthy of remembering them.

Chairman of the Organization of Emigrés of Zbarazh and its Environs

Moshe Sommerstein, lawyer in Israel

———

[Page 19]

Zbarazh
The Landscape of Zbarazh, District of Tarnopol
A Brief Survey of the Jewish Community

The earliest mention of the city of Zbarazh is from the years 1205–1213. It is not known exactly when the city was founded, but there is reason to believe that in 1393 Prince Witold built a fortress on the site.

In 1422, the king bequeathed the city in perpetuity to one of the nobles.

In 1474, Zbarazh went up in flames as a result of Tatar raids, and it again went up in flames at the beginning of the sixteenth century. As a result of raids in the fifteenth century, Prince Zbaraski fortified the city, and in 1629 it had 465 houses.

In 1649, Chmielnicki lay siege to the city. In 1675, the Turks and Tatars conquered the city; again Zbarazh was almost entirely burnt down, and its inhabitants were driven out.

Jews lived in Zbarazh at least as early as the end of the fifteenth century. According to a document from 1593, the cities Stari–Zbarazh and Novi–Zbarazh were leased for three years to Nikolai Yonasowitz and to his partner, the Jew Ephraim Dovid of Novi–Zbarazh, for 9100 gold coins. The lease included the serfs, estates, debts and income.

In the first half of the seventeenth century, the Jewish community in the city grew, and a synagogue was built. However, Chmielnicki's siege in 1649, the Turkish conquest in 1675 and the Haidemak raids in 1708 caused great harm, although the community recovered relatively quickly and the population even increased.

[Page 20]

The community of Zbarazh gained glory from its rabbis. Rabbi Moshe ben Rabbi Lemel Mazel served as the city rabbi during the second half of the seventeenth century (d. 1696). At the beginning of the eighteenth century, the city rabbi was Rabbi Tzvi Hirsch, and in 1920 [sic] Rabbi Shlomo ben Rabbi Yisrael Hacohen Charif. In 1746, Rabbi Alter Teumim, also known as Rabbi Zbarazher, author of *Birkat Avraham*, served as city rabbi.

He was followed by Rabbi Eliezer Rokeach, who passed away in 1754. In 1773, the rabbi of Zbarazh, Rabbi Tzvi Hirsh, son of Rabbi Shimon Bochner, passed away.

Rabbi Aryeh Leibush Berstein ben Rabbi Yissachar–Ber of Brody served as rabbi of Zbarazh, and in 1778 he also served in Brody as the rabbi of Galicia. This post was eliminated in 1786, and Rabbi Aryeh Leibush passed away in 1789. He was followed by Rabbi Shaul ben Rabbi Meir Margulies. After serving as rabbi of Zbarazh, he went to Komarna and Lublin, where he passed away in 1787.

The precious town of Zbarazh–destroyed, desolate and abandoned, without any Jews living in it

[Page 21]

Rabbi Meshullam Feivish Heller (son of Rabbi Aharon Moshe Halevi) took his place and passed away in 1795. He wrote two books: *Derech Emet* and *Yalkutei Yekarim*. Rabbi Yishayahu Braz left the leadership of the rabbinate in Zbarazh and settled in Brody, where he passed away in 1798. In 1800 the *admor* (Hasidic rebbe) of Zbarazh was Rabbi Ze'ev–Tzvi (son of Rabbi Yechiel Michel of Zlotshov). R. Alexander–Sender Margulies was the *av beit din* (chief judge) in Zbarazh and passed away in Satanov in 1862. Rabbi Nachum Halevi Horowitz (son of Rabbi Tzvi) was the rabbi of Zbarazh until he passed away. His place was filled by his son, Rabbi Yaakov Tzvi. In 1840, Rabbi Moshe Yosef (son of Aryeh Leib) Halberstam served as rabbi of Zbarazh. Rabbi Yaakov Tzvi (son of Rabbi Simchah) Babad (1840–1910) was *av beit din* of Zbarazh from 1893 and onward.

Rabbi Yosef (son of Rabbi Moshe) Babad, who was *av beit din* in Tarnopol, also served for a while in Zbarazh. Due to slanderous denunciations, the government expelled him and he served as rabbi in Shniatin in 1842 (d. 1874). He composed *Minchat Chinuch*. R. Gedalia Tzvi Rubinstein became *av beit din* in Zbarazh in 1893, and in 1897 he also became its rabbi. He left behind responsa on *Shulchan Aruch* and a commentary on the Torah.

Rabbi Yom Tov Lipman Halevi Heller was *admor* in Zbarazh and passed away in 1910.

Zbarazh was not only a city of rabbis and Hasidim, but also the city of the first *maskilim* in Galicia. Among them were professionals in free trades: lawyers, physicians, engineers, veterinarians, pharmacists, high government and town officials, officials in various local institutions, and even a Jewish judge.

In 1897, an organization called Hatzionim Hatzi'irim (The Young Zionists) was founded in the city with the goal of raising money to establish a Galician community in the land of Israel. That same year, another Zionistic organization called Achot Tzion (Sisters of Zion) was established in the city. Similarly, at the same time there was also a Yehudah Halevi Organization.

[Page 22]

In 1903 an Igud Nashim (Women's Union) was founded, whose purpose was to advance the learning of Hebrew and Jewish history. In 1904, a Toybi–Ha'aleh club was established, where Hebrew courses were given. That year as well a school based on *Safah Berurah* was active in Zbarazh, where sixty students learned in three classes.

In 1902, the Agudat Dovrei Ivrit (Society of Hebrew Speakers), whose members spoke only Hebrew among themselves, began its activities.

Zbarazh was the birthplace of Velvele Zbarazher (Ehrenkrantz), a well–known folksinger and comedian, and it was also the birthplace of the well–known researcher of Polish literature, Wilhelm Feldman (1868–1919). In 1874, the city was one of 45 whose municipal institutions did not include one Jew. But by 1904 the pharmacist Yaakov Karo was elected Jewish mayor for the third time.

———

[Page 23]

Velvel Zbarazher
Folk–Poet and Troubadour

Yaakov Larens (Peterson, N. Dzsh.) writes: Perhaps you can help fifty–year's reader of the *Forverts* find the source of a song of which I remember a few lines, as we would sing it in my hometown of Lodz:

[Page 24]

Under the earth you will see
Bones lying about without measure.
They were once nicer
Than yours and than mine.

Today, the worms make them their meal.
They are sworn to do so.
Brother, the world is but a dream–
Man was born to die.

Here everything is still, here everyone rests,
Here no one worries,
Here no one needs fine clothing,
Here no one needs to borrow.

Here no one wants sweet food,
No one's ears request music.
Children, the world is but a dream,
Man was born to die.

Here a person sees that he is just a fool,
That all of his logic is foolish.
Here the slave lies next to the master,
The beggar together with the ruler.

Here enemies make peace,
Sworn to each other like brothers.
Children, the world etc.
Under the hills, you will see,

Bones are rotting without measure,
They were also as nice,
And maybe nicer, than yours.
Now the worms make a meal of them,
They are sworn to do that.
Children, the world, etc.

Regarding this song submitted by readers, we have already mentioned on a number of occasions the poet Velvel Zbarzsher (whose real name was Binyamin Wolf Ehrenkrantz), born in Zbarazh in 1826 and died in Constantinople in 1883. Just as various versions are given regarding the exact date of his birth, so too a number of stories and legends have circulated about his interesting life and about his death. (On his tombstone, the year of his birth is given as 1826.) He was fascinated by secular ideas and eagerly read the worldly books of the *maskilim* and of the German classicists. His father wanted to lead him back to the "straight path," and to that end he married him off at the age of 18, and Velvel became a children's teacher. According to one source, his wife was an ignorant girl who could not understand her husband's interest in books and his satiric songs, which he published, but according to another source she was the one who urged him to write and publicize himself. He wrote Hebrew songs, and in order to please his young wife he wrote lyrics in simple Yiddish, "The Hasid and His Wife," composed a melody and sang it to her. Learning of his undisguised heresy, the townspeople persecuted him and forced his father–in–law and mother–in–law to persuade their daughter obtain a divorce from this heretical song writer. He had to flee in 1845 to Rumania, to the Moldavian state of Batosani, where he was a merchant, a school teacher and finally–his true calling–a poet, who loved to sing his compositions over a glass of wine.

[Page 25]

Zalman Reizen writes abut him and about his influence on Jewish life of that time:

Zbarazher was one of the first Jewish folk poets in general and the most significant among the folk poet–comedians, upon whom he had a very great influence. In many of his songs, we find an echo of the ideals of the *haskalah.* In them, he fights against ignorance and credulity, against the Hasidim and holy men, against false piety. There is no bitterness in his anti–Hasidic songs. It is not for nothing that he calls his songs "a pleasant rod"–he struck his targets with compassion. With the help of a fine sense of humor, of colorful, vigorous language, and with the aid of his folksy melodies, he smuggled in his anti–Hasidic tendencies without undermining the religious sensibilities of his listeners. How great Zbarazher's influence on the spiritual life of the Jewish folk classes must have been is indicated not only by the extraordinary popularity of his songs but also by the fact that Zbarazher's popular songs were used as intermission entertainment in texts of traditional Purim plays.

———

[Page 27]

The Lonely Person Wishes to Rest
by Binyamin Wolf Ehrenkrantz
(Velvel Zbarazher)

"Tell me, I ask you, wind,
You sweep across the entire world,
Do you not know where the lonely person can find
A tent in which to rest,
Where murders have ceased,
Where no one ever wailed,
Where no eye ever wept,
Where the righteous person is not troubled?"
The wind is silent and remains still as a stone,
Sighs and answers, "No, no!"

"Tell me, you deep, you great sea,
You whose storms are so far–reaching,
In your islands here and there,
Do you not know any place in some corner,
Where the pious person is consoled,
Where he rests securely?
Do you not know the name of such a town?
Say a good word!"
The sea storms and echoes: "No!
I have not seen such a place."

[Page 28]

"You lovely moon, in your beauty
You oversee everything
Where it is still night,
Covered with a black shawl.
You pass across the entire world,
Always through the nights.
Do you not know somewhere of a tent
Where the good is not bad?"
She can be seen in a passing cloud,
She sighs and answers, "No, no."

"Tell me, my soul's port,
Where are love and hope near?
Where does the sun shine everywhere?
Where does one find a quiet life?
Where is no evil nearby?
Where do we live only in freedom,
Free of sin and worry,

Of troubles and of suffering?" They all give one reply:
"Only in heaven does one live quietly."

from Makel Noam, Vienna, 1865

[Page 29]

Between the Two World Wars

With the Russian conquest in 1914, followed by an interval when Poland and the Ukraine temporarily held power, and then in 1920 under Bolshevik rule, chaos reigned in the city, and Jewish stores were destroyed. However, besides that, the Jews did not suffer particularly from robbery and other acts of violence.

With the installation of the Polish government, those who had collaborated with the Soviets and the Ukrainians fled, and the Polish authorities imprisoned 25 men: Poles, Ukrainians and a number of Jews. Most of these were freed within short order, but three were sentenced to death and were shot in the fields outside the town.

With the abatement of fighting in 1920, the refugees who had fled during the hostilities began to return to the city. In order to help them, an assistance committee was established, one that was particularly active in 1924. Earlier, the six factories in the city had ceased operating. After they were reorganized in 1921, four of these factories were in operation, and the number of those employed was 43. Jewish employees at that time comprised 36.6 per cent of all employees in the city.

From 1928 and onward, a charity fund operated in Zbarazh. In 1929, this fund distributed loans in the sum of 1,1010 [sic] zloty. From 1930, the Union of Cooperatives for Jews in Poland approved credit in the amount of 10,000 zloty for the city's commercial bank.

In 1930, an additional Jewish bank was established in the city, Bank Credit Partners, a successful venture that helped many merchants and artisans.

The charity fund's agricultural activities during period from 1933 to 1937 testify to the financial state of the Jews of Zbarazh.

In 1933–1934, the entire amount of loans was 6,235 zloty. In 1935–36, 89 loans were extended for a sum total of 7,380 zloty, and in 1936–

1937, loans were given to 93 professionals, 126 small merchants, 6 farmers and 45 others.

In 1934, the situation deteriorated, when the city and government imposed heavy taxes on residents, including the Jews. This placed an additional burden upon the Jews' ability to provide assistance for the needy.

In 1935, a children's shelter functioned alongside the local WIZO. The Merchants' Union committee established a special fund to assist its members. In 1939, the Cooperative Bank entered into financial difficulties, which affected its functions and had an impact on those who required its services.

Despite these problems, lively national and public activity took place in Zbarazh.

In 1917, a Hashomer Hatzair branch was founded in Zbarazh, with a membership of hundreds of youths from all strata of the city.

In 1920–21, the first group made *aliyah*. Hashomer Hatzair experienced a brief hiatus, following which it returned to intensified activity. It organized all of the poor of the city. In 1928, a robust division of Gordoniyah (a popular youth pioneer federation) was active, and continued its activities until 1939.

In 1919, a Union of Zionist Women was operating, and in that year a Yardanyah Union of Jewish students was founded. In 1930, a branch of Hashomer Hadati began activities in the city, as did as a number of other organizations, such as the Hebrew Youth (whose name was later changed to Zionist Youth), Akiva and Beitar. In 1934, a vigorous branch of Poalei Tzion was founded, with 70 members.

In 1935, a branch of Achavah was established, with 40 members. In 1939, a branch of Hashachar, a radical Zionist youth movement, functioned in Zbarazh. In the elections for the Zionist Congress in 1935, the General Zionists received 234 votes, Mizrachi 279 votes, and Hitachdut Poalei Tzion 516 votes.

The Role of the Federations

In the elections to the congress in 1939, in practical terms only three large parties kept their power. The General Zionists received 220 votes, Mizrachi received 340 votes and the Working Land of Israel list received 564 votes. The Revisionists received only 140 votes.

Activities in the Municipal Arena

In the municipal and communal arena, whenever city elections drew closer, the Jews of Zbarazh would experience ups and downs.

In 1927, a Jewish bloc called Ichud was established, which included all of the Zionist parties–merchants, artisans, the Mizrachi and even the ultra–Orthodox. Because of the pressure of the local authorities, which issued slanderous fabrications and threats, that year the three national parties lost power and the conservative powers–the National Democrats and the Ukrainian anti–Semites–gained in strength.

In 1931, the situation changed for the better, and a Jew was elected mayor of the city.

But in 1933, the situation again worsened. In the elections to the municipal council, there wasn't even one Jew among the 16 elected. In the elections of 1939, four Jews were elected to the municipal council, in addition to seven Poles and one Ukrainian; however, no Jew was elected to the municipality administration.

Nevertheless, a number of Jews worked in key posts in the municipality.

In the elections to the community council in 1934, as a result of an agreement among all of the parties, the results were as follows: General Zionists–two mandates, Hitachdut–two mandates, Mizrachi–one mandate, Revisionists–two mandates, and Yad Charutzim–one mandate. In the first meeting, Dr. Zindel Segal–a very popular man, a physician–was elected chairman. But the community council did not last long, apparently because of internal difficulties. In June, 1934, it was dissolved by the authorities and a commissary was appointed.

Network of Hebrew Schools and Hebrew Education

During the First World War, a Hebrew school was founded in the city, which most of the Jewish children attended. There were also many *cheders* in which small children learned. However, most of the children learned in Hebrew schools. Besides the schools, there were cultural institutions such as public libraries and a dramatic troupe under the management of Dr. Nissan Speizer. All of this was managed by the Yehudah Halevi Association. There were also kindergartens.

The most important school in the city, which was active for a long period, was the Hebrew institution, Chinuch, which was founded in 1907. This school was highly influential. Most of the Jews in the city, from the assimilated to the ultra–Orthodox, sent their children there. In the morning, the Noar Ha'ivri learned in the general schools and in the Henryk Sienkiewicz Gymnasia, named after the great Polish literary figure. In the afternoon, 520 male and female students (of whom 200 did not pay tuition) learned in the Hebrew school. In addition, evening courses for adults were offered, and there was also a public library. The municipal association, which supported the Hebrew language, was also active in this framework. In the years 1923–1924, courses were offered under the aegis of the Jewish Union for People's Schools and High Schools in Levov. There also existed another two complementary schools, whose financial situation was extremely poor. In 1922, the sports association, Hagibor, was established. It was particularly strong in soccer. The difficult state of the Jews of the city was manifest in the tense relations that existed between the Jews on the one hand and the authorities and non–Jewish residents on the other.

In 1924, the local authorities–in particular, the police– molested the Jews.

Jews were beaten without cause, and a Jewish member of the municipal council, Yaakov Halprin, aged 62, was struck fiercely by hooligans. Finally, the Jews of Zbarazh presented a petition to the Polish Sejm. In 1927, the commissary appointed a governmental official who was known as a blatant anti–Semite, and the head of the district was asked to nullify the appointment.

In 1927, another petition was submitted to the Sejm regarding attacks on the Jews by members of the municipal police. Meanwhile, a local priest conducted anti–Semitic propaganda in the general school.

The Jews of Zbarazh, headed by the city rabbi, asked the mayor to intervene. In consequence, the attacks stopped.

The Second World War

After the outbreak of the war in September, 1939, hundreds of Jewish refugees came to Zbarazh from western Poland, and with the help of the local community they found refuge there.

At that time, there were more than 5,000 Jews in the city.

In autumn, 1939, the activities of the Jewish institutions, political parties and public organizations ceased. That was under the administration of the Soviets, who took control of the city as a result of an agreement between them and the Germans. Governmental institutions (and Polish governance in general) were dismantled and no longer existed. Only the synagogues were not damaged, and the faithful continued to pray there.

Wholesale commerce was liquidated and, after the entire economy of the city was nationalized, retailers gradually closed their stores. Many craftsmen were forced into cooperatives. At the end of June, 1940, many refugees in the city were taken to the Soviet Union. After the German invasion on June 22, 1941, a large group of Jews from the city fled eastward. The Germans entered the city on July 6, 1941. Two days earlier, after the Soviets had left the city, riots had taken place during which a number of Jews had been murdered by the local Ukrainians. The pretext for the riots was the discovery of the bodies of political prisoners who had been killed by the Soviets before their retreat.

Immediately after the Germans entered the city, they murdered a number of Jews in the streets, among them some of the leading citizens of the city: Meir Hindes and his wife, Aharon Klar, Joseph Segal, Israel Sommerstein, and others. The Jews of the city could not even give them the final honor of burial in the cemetery due to the fear of German reprisals, and so they buried them in the large synagogue's courtyard. In the middle of July, 1941, the Germans demanded the establishment of a Judenrat. They turned to past community leaders. However, Zusia Hammer, who had been chairman of the community's committee before the war, refused to accept a position in the Judenrat, citing his poor state of health.

Within a short period of time, Greenfeld, a refugee from western Poland, became head of the Judenrat. From the very beginning, he obeyed the Germans' orders, ignored the interests of the community and acted to its detriment.

On September 6, 1941, Jewish men were summoned to present themselves in the square facing the municipal building. Those who gathered there were surrounded by Ukrainian police and SS units that had come from Tarnopol. A selection was made of 74 men– principally *maskilim* and almost all of the intelligentsia. They were taken to the Lubianki forest, where they were killed and thrown into pits that they themselves had been forced to dig.

In the winter of 1941–1942 and in the spring of 1942, Jewish men were taken from Zbarazh to work camps in the vicinity: Zborov, Kaminka–Stromilova, Borki–Vilki, Halubotzki–Vilki [Lubotzky–Vilki?], Podvolotziskeh [Pidvolochysk?], Maksimovkah, Roznoshenske and Lubianki.

In June, 1942, 600 old and sick people were taken from the city in the direction of Tarnopol and killed. In August 31 and on September 1, 1942, a mass "action" took place, in which a few hundred Jews were sent to be liquidated in the Belzetz camp.

In autumn, 1942, a ghetto was set up in Zbarazh, to which Jews were brought from the nearby communities of Skalat, Hrymayliv (Grzymalow), Podvolotziskeh [Pidvolochysk?] and Nobi–s'olo.

Although the ghetto was not sealed off, the ability to leave it was restricted, and obtaining food was difficult.

The Jews of the city began to prepare hiding places in the ghetto in anticipation of future "actions." They also looked for places to hide in the nearby forests, in "bunkers" and with Christian acquaintances.

By the beginning of October, 1942, few Jews made an appearance in the city.

On October 20–22, 1942, there was another "action," in the course of which more than 1,000 people were rounded up. Many of them were sent to be liquidated in Belzetz, and a group of men was transferred to the Yanovsky camp in Levov.

The process of the destruction of the Jewish community continued on November 8 and 9, 1942. Again, about 1,000 thousand men were taken to Belzetz. Some young people jumped from the moving train, of whom a few succeeded in returning to the ghetto in Zbarazh.

The winter of 1942–1943 saw a worsening of the situation for the survivors in the city. Hunger and illness caused many deaths.

On the other hand, information about German losses on the front encouraged the Jews of the city to bolster their efforts to save themselves. Bunkers were built in the nearby forests, but getting food for an extended period was difficult. Also, the hostile attitudes of the local population made such shelters dangerous. These residents constantly hunted down people hiding in the forests and in pits. Thus, the possibility of being saved in that way was difficult and circumscribed.

The Photostat and the Memorial

On April 7, 1943, more than 1,000 Jews of the city and the surrounding vicinity who were in the ghetto were taken to be killed at a site close to the city.

On June 8, 1943, the ghetto was entirely destroyed. The last of the Jews of the city were killed in mass graves next to the city. Zbarazh was proclaimed *judenrein*. Only small groups of Jews still survived in the surrounding forests, and a handful of Jews hid with gentiles.

Among the gentiles who hid a few of the Jews of Zbarazh, the following should be noted: Joseph Ibshkivitz (in the past, school administrator, died in Auschwitz) and the previous head of the city, Szober. They helped their Jewish acquaintances find refuge in the village of Kartovatzah, and tended to their needs.

But the vast majority of the local residents denounced the hiding Jews and turned them over to the Germans–a phenomenon that continued until the last days of Nazi rule.

In February, 1944, retreating Wehrmacht soldiers came upon Jews of the city hiding in the surrounding villages and murdered them.

On March 6, 1944, the Soviets liberated the city. Among the Jews of the city, only a few individuals were saved. Those who survived left the city for Warsaw, from which they went to the land of Israel and to other countries, such as the United States, Australia, Argentina and Canada.

———

34 Zbaraz Memorial Book

[Page 43]

The Holocaust and the Destruction of the Jews of Zbarazh

This entry appears in English translation at the end of the Yizkor book, starting on page 116.

[Page 83]

On the Path of Suffering
From the Time of the Holocaust in the City of Zbarazh

Sketches

Testimonies

Documents

Protocols

Reportage

Articles

[Page 85]

The Tragic History of Zbarazh, Galicia

(excerpt from an article published in the *Morgn–Journal*, New York 29.1.1948)

by Moshe Sommerstein

Zbarazh, a small town in Galicia, was known as a center of Jewish *maskilim*, with a youth who possessed vigorous national pride: sons and daughters who played an important role in building the land of Israel.

Among the bloody, sorrowful episodes of the destruction of the Jewish people in Poland, Zbarazh too went on the "last road" to martyrdom.

Five years have passed since the days of those bloody slaughters, the so–called "actions."

But this began even earlier. The first victims fell on 9 Tammuz 5701, when the initial squads of the Nazi armies marched across the country. It was a cruel sight when they chose and gathered the leaders of the city, 22 in all. Among these first martyrs were Israel Sommerstein, Aharon Klar, Meir Hindes, Dovid Weihrauch, Israel Kapler, Yosef Segal, Mendel Palyak, Gershon Katz, Mordechai Brell and Israel Rubin. They were buried near the large synagogue, close to the fence.

On 14 Elul, 5701, an order was given for the entire intelligentsia to gather at the city hall. Those who came were immediately surrounded by the stormtroopers. After the murderers set aside the specialists they would need, the victims were taken to the Lubianki forest, where graves were already prepared, and there, after their clothes were torn off, they were all shot.

Among them fell the righteous Rabbi Hillel Sperber, Dr. Halpern, Dr. Goldberg, Dr. Mantel, Dr. Shmeirekh, Professor Zelig Sommerstein, pharmacist Landesberg, Dr. Reuven Herman, engineer Bernstein, and engineer Greenspan.

Dora Sperber, a student and the daughter of Rabbi Hillel Sperber, could not remain silent. When she saw how everyone was being prepared for the mass slaughter, in her wild suffering she yelled, "Murderers, Jewish blood will take vengeance on you!"

She was the first to fall, followed by the other 72 people, the intelligentsia of the town.

However, the painful, terrible days first began with the establishment of the Jewish ghetto in the town.

All of the Jews were expelled from their homes and settled in the small ghetto area, surrounded by a wire fence. Then the Judenrat was created, and everyone began to understand the barbaric plan for liquidation and extermination.

This drove people to seek various ways of rescuing themselves.

People began to build bunkers. They hid in the cellars and in the forests. But the latter did not work, because the Ukrainians collaborated with the Gestapo. Either the Ukrainians delivered the Jews who had run away into the Germans' hands, or else they themselves shot and robbed them. And so, more than 700 people fell in the fields and woods.

The first mass "actions" began on 18 Elul, 5702. 500 people were taken from the ghetto to Belzetz. After that, this became the routine, as it were. On 18 Tishrei, 5703, the worst days began for the Jews of Zbarazh. A group of old Jews was taken away. In the second "action," on 21 Cheshvon, 5703, 1100 Jews were removed from Padvalatshisk [Podvolotziskeh, Pidvolochysk?], Navisyala, and murdered. The scenes of fathers torn from their children and children from their parents were so heartrending that they cannot be described. On 25 Cheshvon, 5703, in the third "action," more than 1,000 Jews were sent to the Belzetz extermination camp.

On 2 Sivan, 5703, the fourth "action" began, bringing an end to the tragedy of Zbarazh.

1,200 Jews were bestially murdered next to the graves of the so–called Neftostroi not far from the new Jewish cemetery. The last death decree was given!

SS men went from apartment to apartment. They destroyed the houses with grenades, thrust the Jews out of their holes and bunkers, pulled the clothes off the victims, and drove them all to the death location, where the wild beasts were already waiting for them, thirsty for Jewish blood.

The day was bright and clear. The sun shone. And on such a day, filled with life, our brothers and sisters were driven–fathers and mothers, children and nursing babies–proceeding on the last three kilometers of the road leading from the ghetto to the place of liquidation.

Steps were cut down into the deep grave so that the victims would feel "more comfortable."

The victims cried out wildly, "*Sh'ma Yisrael*! God, where are You? Save Your people Israel! Have mercy on the innocent children. What have they done wrong?"

These voices mixed with the desperate cries of the children, who had only one word: "Mama! Mama!"

The shooting increased and stopped, the desperate cries were choked and silenced. The only sounds were those of dying and of underground moans and yearning from the murdered in their death throes.

On 6 Sivan, the first day of Shavuos, the last 300 holy martyrs fell on the same site.

May their souls be bound in the knot of life!

Tel Aviv, 21 Cheshvon 5708

[Page 89]

The Yearnings of a Mother
Written in a Bunker in February, 1943
by Sabina Dorfman

My small daughter!
When you needed me, I sent you to strangers.
Forgive me.
I sent you, my child, with my own hands,
Doubting that I would ever see you again.
You stretched your small hand out to me.
"Mama, Mama!" you cried out in tears.
How can I go on living?

We pulled you out of the burning flames.
We decided that we have no choice.
A cruel war, mortar fire,
Most of all, the liquidation of the Jews.
We were without hope,
Buried in the belly of the earth,
Awaiting death, salvation.

If only I had the form of a bird
To enjoy the air, the sun, the light,
To enjoy flying across the sky,
My child, I would come to your windowsill,
To fly around your house
Until I would see your figure.

I would peek through the keyhole,
I would search in the barn, in the coop,
I would hide, I would settle myself
In a corner of the yard,
And no power in the world

Would move me from there.
I would chirp lullabies before you slept,
As in the good old days, in mama's arms.

   Maybe one day you will feel
A trace of love, of yearning.
Maybe, maybe you will recognize my eyes–
Maybe you will caress my wings–
Maybe you will recognize my trembling body,
Sated with joy, sated with fear.
Only then will I grow calm. On my way, I will turn
To help your father, the sentry.

   If, when the cruel war ends,
You do not find your true mother,
Remember, my daughter!
The place that you step upon moist earth
Suffused with tears and Jewish blood.
Remember!
The Nazi monster destroyed
Our lives, hurled them down, ruined them.
It destroyed men, women, children.
The reason for our sin: *we were Jews*.
There is no power of expression in the mouths of human
beings,
There is no power to describe it.
Remember, my child!
One last thing I ask:
Be proud of your Jewish heritage!

———

[Page 91]

Where is the Grave of My Dear Mother?
by Yosef Lilien (from Zbarazh; Bronx, New York, 3.1.1983)

If I were a bird, I would fly over the oceans
To the grave of my dear mother.
I would race a thousand miles to my mother.
The sun would lay down bridges with its brigł
Over rivers, over oceans, to my mother.
The word "mama", like a star, would
Show me the way, so that I would not stray.

And when I arrived,
I would place a wreath on her grave
And I would curse the murderers,
Their hearts hard as stone,
And I would ask the fields:
"Where are the bones?
Oh! You fields, rivers, oceans,
Tell me, where is the grave of my dear mother

[Page 93]

To the Memory of My Dear Parents
Zbarazh Ghetto 1942
by Sabina Dorfman

Only yesterday I saw you, my dear one!
I saw you frightened, weak–
And my dearest father in all the world
Was praying all the time.

Only yesterday, mama, I sat next to you,
I hugged you, I kissed you, I washed your body.
Only yesterday, you held on with the greatest strength.
How everything has gone down to ruin.

My dear papa,
If only I would have known what would happen tomorrow.
Only yesterday in your sad eyes, I saw
Suffering and despair gaze out.

With your sense of humor, clever, learned,
You became a person pained and silent.
Only yesterday, my heart was torn into pieces
To see you both suffer.

If only I could encourage and help
My beloved, pure father.
My dear papa,
If only I would have known that this would happen tomorrow

If only I could see you one more time,
To embrace you, to kiss you, to hear one word.
If only I could cry out loudly,
"Where is the justice? Where is the law?

"Where are the friends? Where is God?
Why is everything still and at peace?"

My dear papa,
If only I would have known what would happen tomorrow.

    I am happy in the present,
I trust in the future,
And I will never forget the past.

———

[Page 95]

I Was the Mother of a Baby
by Sabina Dorfman (from the Folk family)

I was 23 years old, the mother of a nine–month–old baby girl called Tzipporah, a woman in love with a loving husband. With the invasion of the Nazis, our happiness collapsed. We underwent three attacks ("actions") in the Zbarazh Ghetto. In the second, they murdered my parents, Menachem Mendel and Yehudis Folk. They took my firstborn brother, Yishayahu, to the work camp in Levov, where, after he experienced great suffering, they liquidated him.

Lack of hope drove me to give my daughter to a gentile woman married to a Jew in order to save her. Until today, this image haunts me: as she is being handed over, her hands are stretched out to me, and she cries out with tears, "Mama, mama!" This caused me terrible agitation.

I knew that I could not compromise. I must decide: to live or to kill myself. There was nothing in–between. Suddenly, one day I found myself in a paper "shelter." Yes, weak, soft and simple paper. It stood and protected me like a cement wall. It was a wonder drug for the chaos in my brain. I spoke to paper, I wept to paper, I spilled my entire being out on paper.

For over a year, nine people lived in the belly of the ground under terrible conditions: I and my husband Yaakov Lachman (of blessed memory), his sister Leah with her husband Shmuel Chaikin and their daughter Tzila, aged four, two of my sisters, Yaffa, aged 12, and Mina, aged 15, my brother Yitzchak and Malka Folk, who jumped from a death transport. Today we were all underground.

Broken and torn, we were privileged to reach the end of the war. We were privileged to see the downfall of the Nazis–but we did not have the strength to rejoice.

A full month after the liberation of Zbarazh in 1944, our second daughter, Yehudis, was born.

In 1950, we emigrated to the land of Israel. Here we were reborn.

My beloved homeland fully reclaimed me. In it, I found my lost happiness.

———

[Page 97]

A Period of Time
by Ida Fink

I want to tell about a period of time not measured in months. Always, whenever I wanted to tell about this time–and not as I will do now, only about one part of it–I wanted to, but I could not, I did not know how. And I was afraid that this second sort of time, which steals its way into the layers of years (the sort of time that is measured in months and years), would be trampled and flattened within me. But that was not the case. When I recently examined my heap of memory, I found it fresh, not harmed by the disease of forgetfulness. That period of time which is measured not in months but in a word (someone said that it occurred in the lovely month of May). People said that it occurred after the first "action" or after the second, or before the third. We had other ways of measuring time, we who are always different, always branded as being different–which causes some people pride and plunges others into dispirited subjugation. We are responsible for the fact that, due to our being different, we were again judged as we had been before in our history–not just once or twice. Again we were judged during this time that was measured not in months or in weeks, not with the rising of the sun or with its setting, but with a word, with a concept that speaks of movement and deed, a term related principally to literature, to a novel or to a drama. I do not know who was the first to use this word–those who acted or the victims of their actions, the victims of the "action." Who created this technical term that took the place of the earlier term, "manhunt"–a term that, over the course of time, with improved technology, degenerated (or maybe improved?)? The "action" was a manhunt with racial considerations, a manhunt for workers.

The first "action"–that period of time that I want to tell about–we called it a manhunt, although no one hunted and no one was seized. Each one of us delivered himself to imprisonment, although not of his own free will but under orders. One fine, clear morning, in the city square, enclosed within multi–story buildings–a pharmacy, stores for haberdashery and iron, we were imprisoned on the sidewalks with large flagstones that time had split and cracked (after that, I never saw such large stones). In the middle of the square stood the municipal council building, and before that building, we were ordered to stand in rows. *We* were ordered–that is not correct, because *I* did not stand in a row–although, out of obedience to the directive that had been issued the previous evening, I left my house after breakfast, which I ate normally, by the table that was set normally, in a room whose door led to the orchard, wrapped in dry morning mist, gilded by the rising sun. Still we had not changed, still we lived in accordance with the ways of the old time measured by months and years. And that morning was fine and good, filled with pure, golden mist. We read the directive as it was written. And since reading between the lines is not foreign to an adult, we imagined behind the word "work" the image of a work camp–which, it was told, they were setting up near our town. It appears that those giving the directive knew very well the limits of our ability to read between the lines, the limits of our imagination–so impoverished–and so they saved themselves trouble by issuing the written directive. The degree to which they did not err in predicting our response is proven by the fact that after breakfast, which we ate normally, at the table, set as always, the old people in our family decided to ignore the order out of fear that physical work would be too hard for them, but they did not advise the young people to do the same, because the latter would not be able to use the excuse of old age. We lived like infants!

That fine and clear morning sprouts from the heap of my memories still fresh, its colors and smells undiminished: a golden, crisp mist, hanging red apples and a shade over the river, moist and bearing the scent of burdock leaves, and the light blue skirt that I wore when I left the house and when I turned away from the gate. At that moment, it seems, I suddenly passed intuitively from the stage of infancy to the stage of thought, still naïve–intuitively, of course, because I did not think about why I was repelled by the gate that led to the road, and why I chose a roundabout way, through the orchard, alongside the river– "from behind," because it led to the forest thicket–intuitively, because at the time I did not yet know that I would not stand in the square before the municipal building. Perhaps it was because I wanted to delay that moment, and perhaps simply because I loved the river.

On my way, I picked up smooth stones and skipped them across the water. On the bridge, from which the town vista appeared, I sat briefly, I unshod my feet and through their movement I saw my doll's image in the water and the poplars standing on the shore. At that point, I was not yet afraid. Nor was my sister afraid–I forgot to tell that my younger sister went with me. She too sent stones skipping across the water and shook her foot over the river, called the Gneizna, a pathetic stream eight meters wide. She too was not yet afraid. Only after we left the small bridge and, beyond the corner house, the square appeared before our eyes, only then did we suddenly stop, and we did not take another step. The sight that appeared to our eyes had nothing unusual. It was a black crowd, as though on a market day. But it was different, because the market crowd was colorful and loud, the hens crowing, the geese honking, and there was a lively commotion, whereas this crowd was silent, similar perhaps to any other gathering, but also different. The truth is that I don't know. I do know that we stopped suddenly and that my small sister suddenly trembled, and that her trembling affected me as well. She said, "Come on, let's run!" And although no one chased us and the morning continued to be clear and tranquil, we ran back to the small bridge, but we did not see the poplars or the dolls of our images running across the face of the water. We ran for a long time on the steep hill, called Fortress Hill after the ruin of the ancient fortress at its peak, and there, next to this beloved ornament of our town, we sat in the bushes, still panting and shaking. From here it was possible to see our house and our orchard. They were in their place as always. Nothing had changed, including the house of our neighbors, from which the neighbor woman went out and began to beat the rugs. *Tach! Tach!*–the sound of her rug–beater came clearly to our ears. We sat there for an hour, perhaps two hours, I do not know, for time measured in accepted measures ceased to exist. And after we went down the steep hill to the river and returned home, we learned what was occurring in the square and that they had taken our cousin David, how they had taken him and what he wanted to tell his mother, and that he wrote down what he wanted to tell when he was already on his way and he threw a note from the vehicle, which some farmer brought in the evening–but that was later. At first, we learned that they had sent the women home. They told the men alone to remain. And the way in which my cousin went was the opposite of our way. Whereas the sight of the crowd in the square upset us, it attracted him powerfully, overcoming the strength of his nerves, until he himself, as it were, decided his fate–he himself, himself, himself! As he himself wanted to tell his mother, and for which he afterwards wrote: "I myself am guilty. Forgive me."

We never imagined that he was among those who lack equanimity, those whose restlessness and inability to remain still sentence them to destruction–never, because he was fat and rotund, not alert in his movements, someone whom it is difficult to disengage from a book, bent forward, with a stifled laugh like that of a girl. We learned later, much, much later, about his last hours–if they were the last and if they were only hours. Only the end of the war brought us reliable news. The farmer who had brought the note did not dare tell us what he saw–what he himself saw and what others hinted at. No one dared believe it. In fact, they tried to prove that something else was true, indications coming in restricted measure, bit by bit–a version that everyone grasped fervently, a camouflage that was considered to be the entire reality, so much did people work to fool themselves, to pretend to themselves. Only time, the time that is not measured in months and in years, opened their eyes and persuaded them.

Our cousin David left the house later than we did, and when he came to the square, it was already known–not to everyone, but to those called the council, which in the course of time was transformed into the mechanism of the Judenrat–that the words "drafted for work" were not to be interpreted literally. A friend, an old man who foresaw the future, told young David to hide, and since he was too late to go back home, because the roads were blocked, the old man led him to his apartment in one of the stone houses surrounding the square. Since, like us, the old man did not imagine that this youth was among those lacking equanimity, those who have difficulty coming to terms with aloneness and dealing with pressure, he left him in the room, locked with a key. What happened to our cousin enclosed in that room remains forever in the realm of speculation. There is certainly weight to the fact that its window overlooked the square, at that silent crowd, at the faces of those known and close. One may assume that at a certain moment, perhaps in a fraction of a moment, the aloneness that sprouted up from the hiding place to the youth was more onerous than the huge and threatening unknown offered by the world from the other side of the window, the unknown shared by all of those gathered in the square. It was definitely a fraction of a moment, a flash of thought–that he should not be alone but together with everyone else–a movement of the hand was enough. The assumption that he left his safe hiding place because he was afraid that they would search the apartments does not seem right to me. Impatience, nerves, the burden of being alone–these drove him into the abyss of the black crowd. They sentenced him to extermination among the first 71 victims of our town.

He stood in a row between a lawyer's stagiare and an architecture student, and to the question: "Profession?" he replied, "Teacher," even though he had only been a teacher for a short while and by happenstance. His neighbor on his right also did not lie. But the student lied and claimed that he was a carpenter, and that lie saved his life–more precisely, it pushed off the decree of death by two years. 70 of the sort of people called "intelligentsia" were loaded onto vehicles. With that total of 70, the examination ceased. At the last moment, they dragged a rabbi out of the house. He was the seventy–first. As they went to the vehicles, they passed before the rows of those who hadn't had a chance to tell the questioners their type of employment. Then our cousin David said loudly, "Tell Mother that I myself am guilty, and I ask for forgiveness." It appears that already then he did not believe in what we all believed afterwards, which is to say that they were going to a camp. He already had keen vision before his death. The farmer who brought the note in the evening containing the words, "I myself am guilty, and I ask for forgiveness," was gloomy. He did not look into our eyes. He said that he had found the note on the way to Lubianki and that he did not know anything else about it. We knew that he knew, but we did not want to admit it to our own ears. He left, but he returned after the war to tell what he had seen.

A postcard written by the rabbi that arrived two days later persuaded everyone that the 71 expelled people were in a work camp. After a month passed, when the lack of additional news somewhat undermined our faith in a camp, a postcard came written by another one of those expelled, an accountant. With that, the procession of postcards ended. Its place was taken by the giving of gifts to the authorities, who hinted that kilograms of coffee, tea and gold could help a family receive news of their relatives. As an act of kindness, they also allowed sending necessities to prisoners, who–they told–were working in a camp in the area of the Reich. Then, after the second "action," came another postcard, written in pencil, in blurred writing, hard to decipher. After this postcard, we said, "They are being finished off." On the other hand, unsubstantiated rumors passing quickly from mouth to ear told about the boggy ground in the forest near the village of Lubianki and about the handkerchief that had been found, soaked with blood. Those rumors had no owners. There were no witnesses.

That farmer who then did not dare speak came after the war and told us everything. This had happened in the forest that was mentioned in the rumors, a wide, thick forest, not young, five kilometers from town, an hour after the vehicles had left the square. Taking the victims out to be killed took a short while, while the digging of the grave that preceded it took longer.

With the sound of the first gunshot, my cousin, fat and round, not lively in exercise and sport, climbed up a tree. With his arms, like the arms of a child around his mother, he hugged the trunk, and with this he breathed forth his soul.

[Page 105]

From Recollections of the Nazi Conquest
"Action"
by Stella Klinger–Zidenorg (Kiryat Chaim)

At present, in Germany the trial of a few of the tens of thousands of criminals and executioners of human beings is taking place. This trial brings back terrible dreams and dark memories of the cruelest years that mankind has ever known. Wounds that never healed are re-opened. The strongest words and the sharpest pen could not faithfully reconstruct the horrors of those terrible days.

Night in the era of the Nazi conquest–every town has its own story, written in blood. My hand shakes as I write these words, but I will try to describe one of many events that I experienced in the small town of Zbarazh, in the Tarnopol district.

"Action, action!" The terrible knowledge spreads as quick as a flash from mouth to mouth: "action, a–c–t–i–o–n!" To the shelter, to the cellar–to hide, to flee, to remain alive, to be safe! The drive to protect life expressed itself in primitive grasping at the remnant of life. Stubbornly, at the end of our resources, we held firm in order to be safe, in order to live. In seconds, the shelter was full. We heard pounding at the gate: "Open up, Jews, open up!" They knocked and kicked until the gate burst under the wild pressure. We did not move, as though we were dead. It seemed as though my heart had stopped. Through the small cellar windows came the despairing voices of the first who were seized in the "action."

"Jews, where are they taking us, to slaughter?" Children were given a double portion of Luminal so that they would be calm and silent. In the shelter adjoining ours, a crying two–year–old girl was choked, the daughter of Melly and Robert. 26 people were saved. Every day we gave the babies and small children the poisonous but silence–inducing Luminal. The shelter was so tightly closed that there was no air. The ventilators were of no use. Women lay on each other, faint. "Water,

water, help!" white lips whispered. Small children vomited in their sleep. The "action" continued. I felt as though I was in a submarine that has dived and cannot be recovered. Around us, bits of drama occurred. Young people embraced and separated, sent last instructions. "If one of us stays alive … if you live … remember … do not forget." Lack of air, faces covered with sweat. Someone yelled: "Open up the shelter! If this goes on, we will all choke!"

A pious old man recited a blessing, whispered the confession. 36 hours in this shelter, an eternity!

Everyone held his breath: can it be? A sound of weeping that had been withheld for so long broke forth from our throats, like an echo bouncing off the walls and rising, rising, it seemed, to heaven. In the underground shelter, we heard the noise of vehicles driving away. The criminals were leaving the city.

They returned to Tarnopol. It was enough for the day. The harvest of death was rich. But they did not discover our shelter. Wrung out, despairing, with sad faces, we emerged. We dragged our children on the steps like packages. The Luminal was still at work. The children's faces were white, tired, frightened, the faces of small victims, children who were grown before their time, knowing and understanding everything. My oldest son, the first–born, asked: "Mother, how long have I been alive?" "Seven years, my son." "Mother, then it is wonderful that I have lived at least seven years!" Tears choked me. Something wept from within. Something was torn–"mother," a Jewish mother! How much despair and despondency in these words. I will cover my children with my body but will I manage to protect them, will I succeed in guarding them? It is so easy to die and so hard to protect another day of life. The battle takes place for every day, every moment.

Another "action," and they discovered all of the shelters. There was no longer safety in a shelter. At night, we fled to the forest. Quickly, more quickly, so that no one would see us. Early in the morning, the shining head of a animal appeared in the wet grass. A snake? Perhaps it is venomous? I stepped backward in fear. "Mother," whispered my small son, seven years old. "What are you afraid of? That isn't a person!" Fate was friendly, and death did not want me.

Like the fragments of a ship that has broken up, we miraculously remained alive. Joy was always hidden from our hurting hearts, because the shadows of our brothers, sisters and parents remained in them. Belzetz, Lubianki, Yabovke, Paviak, Choloth–that was our common denominator. One big graveyard.

Now we live in Israel under the light of the sun and in the freedom of our homeland, but the horror of the night of the Nazi conquest exists within us. The shadows of our persecuted and worn–out relatives, never forgotten, live within us. In their name, on behalf of the injustice done to them, we cry out for vigilance and for justice.

———

[Page 109]

The Might of the Jews of Zbarazh
by Zalman Rosenberg

During the bloody days when the Nazis ruled our town, our brothers and sisters were filled with might in facing the enemy and murderer.

As soon as Hitler's gangs entered the town, and after the first blood bath that they perpetrated in the Jewish streets, they told the heads of the community to gather together: the leaders of the Jewish populace and the religious leaders with Rabbi Hillel Sperber (of blessed memory) at their head. These numbered 71, like the 71 members of the Sanhedrin. The enemy's goal was known. Those who gathered together knew what awaited them and that their hours were numbered. And here appeared the pride of the rabbi of Zbarazh.

Rabbi Hillel Sperber: who doesn't remember that tall Jew with the white, patriarchal beard and clever eyes? His congregation loved him, and he was mentioned with respect among the Christian populace. Legends were told of his wisdom. When a Jew and a Christian had a dispute, or even two Christians, they went to the rabbi to adjudicate the case, because they knew that he would issue a ruling as fit and correct as that of the government. So, as said, the rabbi was known in all areas. He was so great that we had to share him with the community of Zlotshov; he dedicated three days of the week to Zlotshov and four days to our town. Leaders of Christian persuasion came to him with various problems, and in his wisdom he answered them. And in this way he attained a great reputation.

Peasants who were present at the "action" told that when the Germans–may their name be blotted out–gathered the 71 people with the rabbi at their head, before they sent them away to liquidate them, a priest came to the gathering place and asked the SS leader to spare the rabbi. But before the murderer answered, the rabbi called out proudly (as it is written in the holy books), "Wherever the flock goes, there goes the shepherd." And away went the shepherd with the flock, and they were brutally murdered. They were buried alive in a depression in the Lubianki woods. The peasants told that for the next few days the soil moved over their tormented bodies. May the memory of our leaders with the rabbi at their head never be forgotten.

Three youths showed great courage, going went in the direction of Volhin–Palesia in order to report if it was possible to join the partisans in those forests. Sadly, this attempt failed. The distance was too great and the road was under surveillance. As the youths were on the way, they were captured, and their young lives were cut short.

How much strength did our mothers and wives display! Leaving the ghetto, they went to the villages to get a loaf of bread for their sons and husbands, who languished in the forced labor and extermination camps. More than one woman paid with her life for her sacrifice.

It should be written down so that it will never be forgotten: the account of a man who was in a forced labor camp in Luzov, near Tarnopol. He, with everyone else, worked–and starved–digging sand. These men loaded sand and stones onto train wagons. This was Mekhl Hecht, a resident of Zbarazh, a Jew who, in happy times, throughout the year earned a living carrying water for the residents, just like Y. L. Peretz's Bonche Schweig. Whether or not he was paid, he brought water into people's homes. He languished in the Luzov camp together with everyone else in sweat and in blood, barely standing on his feet. Under a commando, they gathered stones and filled buckets of sand. The bloodthirsty volksdeutsch Ostrovsky was the supervisor. His pleasure lay in splitting open the heads of Jews. Not a day went by that one of us did not fall soaked with blood. With utter cruelty, the murderer turned his attention to Mekhl Hecht. As mentioned, Mekhl could not bear to see his fellow–townsmen suffering–not only from hunger but also of thirst at the backbreaking labor of digging sand. He could not supply them with bread, because he himself was starving, but there was a great deal of water in the village. But the degenerate volksdeutsch did not allow it to be brought. So the weak Jew Mekhl, despite being warned, sneaked out and brought water to the weak. For a long time he succeeded, but one time the murderer noticed that the small zshidek was missing. He ran to the village and caught him there. The entire way from the village to the sand–digging site, he struck the weak Jew in the back with a stone. At the digging site, he pushed him and cast him twenty meters down into the pit. Falling down onto the sand, he still groaned, and here the murderer mutilated his body before the eyes of all of the tormented prisoners. At night, a few youths risked their lives to bury the martyr in the field. No doubt the grave was uprooted so that not a remnant remained, but in the memory of the few survivors he will remain a hero and will never be forgotten. There were many such silent heroes in our town, and Mekhl Hekht is mentioned as a representative of those who sacrificed their lives to help others.

Our town and its environs produced very prominent doctors and teachers. They were active in Zbarazh and many brought light to other towns as well. Two of them may serve as an example.

Yitzchak Kofler was born in Zbarazh, studied and then was a director in a school in Bezhezine near Lodz. Because of his abilities, he was selected as head of that town's community. And he did not forget his birthplace. During the time of turmoil, he and his family returned to Zbarazh, from which the Nazis sent them away to be murdered in Belzetz.

A second Zbarazh resident was Reuven Rosenberg. He had a university education and spoke 12 languages perfectly. He had a post as teacher in the government gymnasium in Stavibsk near Kalna. With his scholarship, he could have climbed much higher. However, the anti–Semitic authority looked with a jaundiced eye on a Jew occupying such a position, and demanded that he either convert to Christianity or leave his position. The talented professor did not abandon his faith over his career. He proudly left the foreign camp and dedicated his life to the Jewish children in Tarbut school (Suwalki) and in Talmud Torah (Visnyuvtze). He wrote poems about Jewish life in Poland and–because he was an enthusiastic Zionist–about the pioneers. These were published in Jewish newspapers in Polish. Tragically, they were destroyed together with the author. In order to give a sense of the mentality of a Zbarazh intellectual, below are a few stanzas from a poem written by this professor–lines that were carved into my memory.

Exile's Plagued Our Tribe, Our Brothers
Translated from the Polish by Dobrochna Fire

Exile's plagued our tribe, our
brothers
For two thousand years and moı
From the bloody times of Titus
Butchers have on us made war

When fierce knights in middle ages
Fought to win the Holy Land,
Swords were honed on Jewish bodies,
Bulwarks built of Jews, not sand.

[Page 114]

Let us finally halt misfortune;
Enough of blood and tears and pain.
Our suffering will find an ending
In a country free and born again.

———

[Page 115]

Israeli Witnesses Face to Face with the Murderer of Tarnopol Jews
Translated from the Polish by Dobrochna Fire

12 Israeli citizens flew to Austria yesterday to give testimony in the trial of Friedrich Lachs, the murderer of Tarnopol Jews.

Lachs's trial started on Tuesday in Gratz, eliciting great interest because the court in this same city last year acquitted another criminal, Franz Murer.

The 53-year-old Lachs is accused of active participation in the extermination of 70 thousand Galician Jews in the period from April 1942 to June 1943, when he headed the Sonderdienst in this region. He is also accused of personally murdering 13 Jews.

On Thursday, Lachs's former supervisor, Herman Miller, in his testimony claimed that the Judenrat in Tarnopol had itself appealed to the Germans with the request to "liquidate" numerous sick Jews in the ghetto.

After the war, Lachs was in hiding in Austria, but he was unmasked thanks to the actions of the division for pursuing Nazi criminals under the main command of the Israeli police.

One of the witnesses was Gerszon Landsberg, who works in this division and who had spent time in the Tarnopol ghetto.

[Page 116]

Nazi Criminals Receive Life Sentences
Stuttgart, 15 (Palestine Telegraphic Agency)

Two of the principal defendants in the trial of the murderers of the Jews of Tarnopol, Herman Miller, aged 57, and Paul Robel, aged 60, were sentenced on Friday in Stuttgart to life imprisonment with hard labor.

Among the ten defendants, five others were sentenced to prison sentences ranging from two–and–a–half years to ten years, whereas three others were acquitted due to lack of proof.

———

[Page 117]

Witnesses from Israel at the Trial of the Nazi Laks

Sergeant Major G. Landsberg, who brought about the capture of the Nazi criminal P. Laks, left yesterday at the head of a group of ten witnesses from Israel in order to appear at the trial of the lieutenant commander of the SD in the Tarnopol vicinity in Galicia during the war.

Laks's sentence began to grow clear in the city of Graetz, Austria, at the beginning of the week. The Israeli witnesses will appear during the trial. Laks, who is considered responsible for the deaths of 80,000 Jews, is accused of the murder of thirteen Jews with his own hands. He was responsible for the local Gestapo's Jewish division and served as Eichmann's representative.

Sergeant Major Landsberg, who was sent by the Israeli police force's Division to Investigate Nazi Crimes to trace the steps of the criminal, found him in 1960 working in a Catholic church in Graetz, and brought about his imprisonment.

Laks's commanding officer, the head of the Gestapo in Tarnopol, Herman Miller, and 22 of his aides will be brought to trial in September of this year in Stuttgart, Germany.

———

[Page 118]

My Little Town
by Moshe Speiser (New York)

Zbarazh, my little town,
Zbarazh, my little home,
Where my cradle stood,
Where I went to *cheder*.

From this small, out–of–
the–way town,
My relatives went,
Driven away by murderers.
Only graves remain.

The little town is no
more.
The pain is great.
Crushed by Nazis,
Choked in gas chambers,

Chased and pursued,
Those who remained alive,
All of their hope is in ruins,
Everything was covered by
the earth.

———

[Page 119]

Berta–Batka Rosenstraukh–Goldwasser
(of blessed memory)

Berta, born in 1932, lived in Paris and was married to Aaron Goldwasser, a Jewish sculptor. They had an infant. The husband and infant perished. She jumped from a train car, was cared for by nuns, and volunteered for the Resistance. She received many outstanding citations for her dedicated service in the French underground.

After the war, in 1949 she moved to Argentina and established a new family. The couple had an only daughter, who is at present married to an Israeli, a professor in the University of Krakas [sic].

[Page 120]

The Holocaust
by Moshe Sommerstein (Tel Aviv, 5743–1983)

1

Krystallnacht, 1938,
And the bitter year of 1940,
All mankind trembled.
The Holocaust began.

2

Days of threats and worries
Days of rape and
persecution,
Days of uproar and
trembling.
The Holocaust began.

3

The days of the Second
World War
Into which all Europe was
dragged,
Country after country
conquered.
The Holocaust began.

4

Every city, town and village
Went up in fire and in ash,
Refugees on dirt roads.
The Holocaust began.

5

Fleeing on the way, which
was no way,

Men, women and children,
From every place and city.
The Holocaust began.

6
Crowded roads and trains,
Crowded cars and wagons,
All of them going east.
The Holocaust began.

7
And the faces of everyone
anxious,
And all of them seized by
trembling.
Has the end of the world
arrived?
The Holocaust began.

8
And the refugees feeling
That their days had ended,
That their tongues were
stilled,
That the Holocaust began.

9
Thousands upon thousands
of our people were split
open,
Rivers of blood of our
fathers poured forth,
Bodies and corpses were
burned
In the fiery ovens, they were
silenced.

10
The Nazis' rampage ended,
The work of bitter horror,
The wretched in the camps
of the savages roared.
The Holocaust continued.

11
Judaism was destroyed,
Life was stilled
In water and in fire,
In choking and in auto de
fas,
In gas ovens,
In bunkers and in fields,
In forests and in ghettos,
Everything rose in smoke
and in uproar,
And no memory remained of
the vile deeds,
Because the Holocaust
ended.

12
And with the passing of
days, today and tomorrow,
And in all of the days, in the
present and future,
The nation will remember
the unjust hatred,
The nation will remember
the valley of weeping,
It will not forget any of the
distress.
The pain and the suffering

will remain forever.

Therefore, remember, remember, that which Amalek did to you, forever!

———

[Page 123]

Translations from the German by Osnat Ramaty

Protokoll.

Es erscheint die röm-kat. Nonne der Felicianerinnen
Maria und gibt an:
Vor dem röm-kat Kindergarten wurde am 14.11.42. abends
gegen 10 Uhr ein etwa 1 Jahr altes Kind, weiblichen Ge-
schlechts in einem Sack verpackt, gefunden.
Ich neige zu der Ansicht, dass es ein jüdisches Kind ist.
Ich bitte um Entscheidung, was mit diesem Kind geschehen
soll.

Zbaraz, den 16.11.42.   V.u.g.

Generalgouvernementt
Kreishauptmannschaft Tarnopol
Der Landkommissar in Z b a r a z .

An den
Kommandeur der Sicherheitspolizei
Aussenstelle Tarnopol.

vorstehendes Protokoll übergebe ich mit der Bitte
um Entscheidung, was mit diesem Kinde geschehen sollte.
Die Ansicht der röm-kat. Nonne Maria , dass das Kind
eine Jüdin ist scheint mir richtig, da mir gemeldet
wird, dass eine Jüdin, deren Name leider Festgestellt
nicht festgestellt werden kann , bei einzelnen Bauern
ein Kind angeboten hat und 20.000 Zl. für die Aufnahme
des Kindes zahlen wollte. Die Bauern haben das Ansuchen
abgelehnt. Ich versuche von hieraus festzustellen, in welchem
Dorf dieser Vorgang stattgefunden hat.

Der Landkommissar

Protocol

The Roman Catholic nun Maria of the female "Polizianer" appeared and declared:

In front of the Roman Catholic nursery, on the 14th of November 1942, a female child, about one year old, was found around 8 pm. She was wrapped in a bag.

I tend to believe that it is a Jewish child. I would like you to clarify what should happen with this child.

Zbaraz, 16th of November, 1942

Read and authorized (by)
(Signature)

General government
District Office (of) Tarnopol
The country commissioner of Zbaraz

To the commander of the security police
Branch office (of) Tarnopol

I surrender the above protocol with the request to decide what should happen with this child. The opinion of the Roman Catholic nun Maria that the child is a Jewess seems to me to be correct. I was told that a Jewess whose name can't be identified, offered a child to a few different farmers. She wanted to pay 20,000 zloty for the them to take the child into their

homes, but the farmers refused. I'm trying
to determine in which village this process
took place.

The country commissioner

[Page 124]

I B=F. 57   40

Gend.-Posten Zbaraz
Kreis Tarnopol
Distrikt Galizien   Zbaraz, den 19.August 1942.

Nachweisung.

Über die z. Zt. beim Gendarmerie-Posten Z b a r a z

tätigen Juden und Jüdinnen.

Lfd. nr.	Zu-und Vornamen	Geb.Datum u. Ort		Wohnort
1.	Stiefel Johann	13.5.34	Krasno	Zbaraz, Szewczenka 4
2.	Segall Osias	1.6.06	Zbaraz	" , ru-Olgi 20
3.	Landesberg Mendel	24.12.87	"	" , Szewczenka 6
4.	Brandes Xaier	2.8.95		" , Ravajdacol 2
5.	Witriol Salomon	20.11.85	Tarnopol	" , Krausa 3
6.	Winograd Benjamin	26.12.13	Zbaraz	" , Kruta 57.
7.	Gottreich Oskar	25.8.23	Krakau	" , Zajeczkiwski 86
8.	Steiner Ferdinand	8.1.33	Puchow	" , Hitlerplatz 34
9.	Kahane Rolf	24.3.37	Zbaraz	" , 6 lstostr.41
10.	Fradis Joseph	6.5.01		" , Lubowycra 3
11.	Weigler Osiasen	24.12.87	Ternopol	" , Hitlerplatz 35
12.	Lilein Leib	6.1.03	Zbaraz	" , Ku.Mazepa 6
13.	Goldberg Rosa	8.1.01		" , Mazepy 20
14.	Nussbaum Berta	25.7.14	Nastasow	" , Seistoniuwa 23
15.	Dubener Zuzanna	9.1.27	Triest	" , Michnowskoho 25
16.	Segall Dorota	12.1.15	Krasno	" , Szewczenka 14
17.	Sonne-Feigenbaum Sala	14.7.24	Tarnopol	" , Krausa 6
18.	Gastfreund Fena	19.7.24	Dubowce	" , Byuldacinaho 34
19.	Pesranik Guste	30.1.21	Zbaraz	" , Michnowskoho 1
20.	Schapu Laura	22.5.23	Zbaraz	" , Hitlerplatz 75
21.	Kronengold Lyda	10.2.12	Krakau	" , Dorozicka 7
22.	Teglaler Anna	6.5.25	Zbaraz	" , Hitlerplatz 23
23.	Kahane Laura	23.7.23	Tarnas	" , Wilson-Pan. 57
24.	Waltuch C.la	2.7.06	Zbaraz	" , Hitlerplatz 18
25.	Silber Klara	2.5.20	Zbaraz	" , Lesi Ukrai.ki 37
26.	Blau Hela	29.3.21	Prudnik	" ,
27.	Goldrosen Amala	6.6.09	Zbaraz	" , Hitlerplatz 7
28.	Guslimann Mina	25.6.14	Gajuatow	" , Kocowalca 6
29.	Landesberg Sala	25.8.17	Zbaraz	" , Sicokienka 8
30.	Nussbaum Anna	21.4.35	Tarnopol	" , Kocowalca 50
31.	Schwajuk regina	23.8.21	Zbaraz	" , Murka 15
32.	Kornberg Musia	27.7.25	Zbaraz	" , Lubowycra 5
33. F	Fisch Estera	13.7.04	Zbaraz	" , Lesi Ukrainki 10

Erklärung: Ständig tätig sind: Lfd.Nr.1 als Bursche u.Pumpenwart
     " " 2 u.3 als Holzhacker
    Vorübergehend tätig sind: Lfd.Nr.6u.7. als Maler, Gend.Unterkunft
         " " 4,5,8-12 als Hilfsarbeiter bei
                Pferdestallsbau
         " " 13-33 als Hilfsarbeiterinnen
                 im Garten u.auf d.Fsld.

Die hier vorübergehend tätigen Juden und Jüdinnen werden dem Arbeitsamt
nach beendigung ihrer hiesigen Beschäftigung zum Einbau zur Verfügung
gestellt.

               Hauptmeister der Gendarmerie
               u. Gend.Postenführer

               /Krützfeld/

Gendarmery Guard Zbaraz
District of Tarnopol
District of Galicia

Zbaraz, 19th of August, 1942
Certificate

Evidence of the Jews and Jewesses currently
the Gendarmery Guard (of) Zbaraz

No.	Surname	First name	Birth date	Birth place	Residence in Zbaraz
1	STEIFEL	Johann	13.5.1924	Krosno	Szawaczanka 4
2	SEGALL	Osias	1.6.1906	Zbaraz	Ha-Olgi --20
3	LANDESBERG	Mendel	24.12.1907	Zbaraz	Szawaczanka 6
4	BRANDES	Koler	02.02.	Zbaraz	
5	WITRIOL	Salomon	20.11.1903	Tarnopol	Krausa 23
6	WINOGRAD	Beniamin	25.12.1918	Zbaraz	Kruta 57
7	GOTTREICH	Oskar	25.02.	Krakau	Zajaczkiwski 85
8	STEINER	Ferdinand	05.01.	Puchow	Mitlerplatz 5a
9	KOHANA	Wolf	24.03.97	Zbaraz	S iatorstr.41
10	PRADIS	Josef	06.06.1891	Zbaraz	Lubowycza 3
11	WEIGLER	Osiason	24.10.1897	Tarnopol	Mitlerplatz 38
12	LILEIN	Leib	06.01.1902	Zbaraz	Ka.Homona 6
13	GOLDBERG	Rosa	08.01.1891	Zbaraz	Mazopy 20
14	NUSSBAUM	Berta	25.07.		23
15	DUBENER	Zuzanna	09.01.1927	Triest	Michnowskoho 25
16	SEGALL	Dorota	12.01.1915	Krosno	Szowezenka 14
17	SOHNEREIGENBAUM	Sala	14.07.1924	Tarnopol	Krausa 6
18	GASTFREUND	Pena	19.07.1924	Dubowce	
19	PECZENIK	Gusta		Zbaraz	Micnowskoho 1

20	SCHAPU	Laura	22.05.1923		Mitlernplatz 75
21	KRONENGOLD	Lyda	10.02.1912	Krakau	Doronzocka 7
22	WECHSLER	Anna	06.05.	Zbaraz	Mitlerplatz 23
23	KAHANO	Laura	23.07.1923	Zbaraz	Hilasa-Pan 27
24	WALTUCH	Gala	02.07.	Zokraz	Mitlerplatz 18
25	SILBER	Klara	2.09	Zbaraz	Lesi Ukrai Ki 37
26	BLAU	Hela	28.03.1921		Lesi Ukrai Ki 37
27	GOLDROSON		06.06.	Zbaraz	Mitlerplatz 7
28	GUELEMANN		23.08.1912		Konovalca 6
29	LANDESBERG		23.08.1917	Zbaraz	
30	NUSSBAUM		22.06.1928	Tarnopol	Konozalca 58
31	SCHWAJUK	Regina	28.08.1928	Zbaraz	Wurka 15
32	KORNBERG	Nusia	27.07.1925	Zbaraz	Lubowycza 5
33	FISCH	Estera	15.07.09--1904	Zbaraz	Losi Ukrainki 10

Explanation: serial numbers 1 are permanently working as an errand boy (messenger) and as a waterman (pitman),
Serial numbers 2 and 3 as woodcutters.
Serial numbers 6 and 7 are temporarily working as a painter, ??,
Serial numbers 4, 5, 8 – 12 are working as auxiliary workers in the construction of horse stables,
Serial numbers 13 – 33 are [female] workers in the garden and in the field.

The Jews and Jewesses will be transferred to the employment office after they complete their temporary work here working on the railroad.

Main Protector of the Gendarmery
and Gendarmery Guard
/Krützfeld/

[Page 125]

Neftostroi

by Yosef Lilien (from Zbarazh; the Bronx, New York, 3.1.1983)

A grave of a thousand victims.
In the middle of the field stands a stone.
Breeze, carry my thoughts,
I will not forget what happened.
Fly, breeze, fly to my little town.
For you, there is no border, no wall.
There, where my dear ones are lying,
Carry my hurt, carry my sorrow.
Tell the souls about my great pain and my lament.
And for the innocent victims, recite the Rabbanan Kaddish!
Fly, bird, good brother,
And when you get to Zbarazh,
Place my sorrowful song on the grave
Like a wreath of flowers!

———

[Page 127]

The Battle for Redemption in the Land of Israel

Our townspeople recorded magnificent pages in *aliyah*, in labor, in settlement and in all aspects of the development of our land.

This began in the 1920s, when a large group made *aliyah*. Most of them settled in the kibbutzim of Tel Yosef and Ein Harod.

After that came a second group in the years 1926 and 1936. And afterwards came the group of pioneers from Gordonia. They too settled in the kibbutzim and kevutzot (communes): Nir Am, Mizra, Mishmarot, Kiryat Anavim and other places.

Most of them joined the defensive forces.

This column will note a few of the people of Zbarazh who are no longer alive but who gave their strength, energy and even their blood for the sake of redeeming the nation and the land.

———

[Page 129]

Letter to a Friend

From a letter of Israel Harodi–father of Chaim–to Yehudah Raznitshensko, who dedicated his composition, *The Third aliyah*, to Chaim's memory

...In those days, shortly before Chaim was born, conditions in Tel Yosef were not particularly congenial for women in childbirth, and even less so in the hospital in lower Ein Harod.

I took Chanah to the hospital a number of times, but after a day or two she returned shamefaced, because the female medic had said, "You were a little early, you were too hasty!"

As I recall, the last time I went to the stable to harness a pair of animals to take Chanah to the hospital, I didn't find a harness. That was on the Sabbath. The wagon drivers had apparently hidden the harnesses to keep anyone taking out their animals, because animals too need to rest on the Sabbath. Only one harness was in its place–that of the horses Saadia and Lotus. I harnessed them and held the reins to take them out of the stable, but they didn't move. I pulled and pulled, but all of my efforts were in vain. I was about to give up when an acquaintance came to the barn and pointed out that their legs were hobbled by being locked to a pole–something that I hadn't noticed. I ran here and there until I got the key. The next day, the secretariat was informed that there was no suitable place in the hospital for women in childbirth, and that if we wanted Chanah to give birth there, we ourselves must supply a proper shed. At that time, Sh. K. lived in a small, light shed. At my request, he moved elsewhere. I took apart his shed and loaded it onto the wagon. With the help of one of the wagon drivers, I got hold of various work tools. I flattened a patch of ground near the patients' ramshackle building and I began to set up the walls. When I was almost finished, the female medic came to me and told me that my wife had given birth to a boy and that I must run to Tel Yosef and bring a Primus stove to heat the water, because they did not have a working Primus.

I had son....

At first, I ran for some distance as I reviewed the medic's words: "Your wife gave birth to a son. You need to bring a Primus stove."

For some reason, I ran across the fields and not on the road fully along the length of the Gilboa. Little by little, I forgot why I was moving. I only knew that I needed to run. As I ran, I began to compose songs out of deep happiness and joy. These songs–where did they come from? I don't think that I had ever heard them. They were created as I ran. I came to the swampy area, quite far from Tel Yosef. I sank into the mud, but to the beat of the song I skipped and leaped from one dry spot to another. The day set. Dusky shadows. The last rays of the sun reflected off the swamp puddles. The silence that grew and took over enveloped me. Everything was blended into great happiness. The Gilboa was the sole witness of my joy, and so I was not embarrassed, but I leaped and sang. Without noticing it, I approached the kibbutz.

The lights in the long stables reminded me about the Primus stove. The wagon drivers in the stable laughed to hear my request ... a Primus stove! They also laughed at my mud–covered face and soaked and filthy clothes and shoes.

"Look at the celebrant...."

And they brought me the Primus.

**

23 years passed (more precisely, minus seven days).

That Sabbath, I was with my brother in Ein Shemer. From the noonday radio news, I learned about searches in Tel Yosef and about the murder of Hodi ... and that there were roadblocks.

Right after that I tried twice to get away from my brother and brother–in–law so that I could walk home by way of the mountains. But they clung to me and brought me back to the kibbutz. Toward evening, however, I accompanied the local mukhtar to the beginning of Wadi Ara. The mukhtar asked the officer on guard to take me in the car that would be traveling in the direction of Tel Yosef. During the hours that I waited for the car and then as I traveled, dark thoughts assailed me. "Chaim, Chaim!" Thoughts about him drilled through my mind without cease. "But why must it be Chaim? There are hundreds of Jews in Tel Yosef. I had wanted to telephone him to come to Ein Shemer for the Sabbath. Why didn't I do it? No! It is not Chaim." It was growing dark when I entered the armored car. The officer, who spoke German to me, told me that he was traveling in the direction of Tel Yosef. Five armed soldiers were sitting in the car. It traveled quickly, for about twenty minutes. I felt that I was reaching my goal. I wondered if I were hurrying home only out of my worry for Chaim, or because of my worry for the kibbutz, for my friends. I had no doubt whatsoever that if Chaim had been with me in Ein Shemer, we would have traveled in this way together, despite all of the difficulties.

Suddenly, the car stopped. A convoy of cars rushed toward us. In their faint headlights I could distinguish the Jewish youths with white and tired faces who were standing in the vehicles. The convoy flew by. The officer said something to the driver, and our car joined the convoy. The car traveled quickly, and as it did it struck another military car and threw it a distance of a few meters beyond the culvert. We stopped. Everyone in our car was all right. One after another, the soldiers said, "We were lucky." I don't know what happened to the people who were traveling in the car that turned over, nor were the soldiers traveling with me interested in their fate.

This incident delayed us for an hour. I looked toward the mountains of Ephraim shadowed in the dark. I was apathetic about the incident that had occurred, but I felt that I didn't want to tell myself, "We were lucky."

"My dear Chaim! Why were you so faithful?" I said to myself.

"But how do you know that Chaim was killed? Why would it be Chaim? "Why? He always said that he wouldn't allow himself to fall into their hands." And again: "But there was no organized opposition; was this just some fatal accident?"

I didn't notice when the car turned east and traveled in the direction of Tel Yosef. I was surprised to see where we were. The soldiers appeared to be irritated. I wanted to ask a question, but something stopped me.

And again I rebuked myself: "You wanted things to be like this. You educated him in your spirit. Why did you only think about yourself and not about his life? But certainly nothing has happened! Chaim is alive, he is in detention together with his comrades. He certainly followed directions together with everyone else. He followed orders.

"So why are you making yourself suffer when you don't know for sure that it is he who was killed? You will do better to stop thinking. Soon you will come home, and you will see that that there is no basis to your fears."

The car came to Afula. When we passed the brightly lit town teeming with couples strolling and happy young people in the streets, I felt better. I showed the driver which direction to drive in. Now I felt at home. The Gilboa was to my right. This mountain that crouches to the length of the valley, crowded with the weight of generations and events, looked at me at this hour, steeped in its silence.

The soldiers had apparently had fallen asleep. Even the officer sitting next to the driver had lowered his head as though he was dozing. Only I stood on my feet and forced all of my being to focus on receiving news. I turned around. Unwittingly, my hand touched the submachine gun of a soldier who had fallen asleep. "Pick it up and put an end to everyone in the car!" I heard a voice. My hand touched the gun bolt. I grew tense. "You are mad, what are you doing? ... But they killed Chaim. ... You are mad! How do you know that it is Chaim who fell? ... But what difference does it make? And what do you have to lose?

"But it is not possible that Chaim is no longer alive.

"And why do I deserve such a thing? Why am I guilty? And what was the guilt of my Chaim?"

The car stopped next to the road going up to Tel Yosef. I jumped out and began to run. After I had gone a few meters, I realized that I had veered left off the road. I wanted to turn back to the road, but for some reason I was unable to. I went on to the culvert, and alongside it I felt myself falling.

I bent my knees and leaned on my hands on the ground. I felt that I was about to sink down onto it. I aroused myself and got up. "What's with me? What has happened to me?" I ran a few more steps and again fell. This time I knew that Chaim is no more.

I got up slowly. Dark and quiet around me. Before me, a short way home. I walked slowly. A little more and I was in the kibbutz. But it was very strange: in all of the kibbutz houses there was no light except in the office and in my room. "And why is the light on only in my room?" When I entered, I saw Chanah looking at me quietly. Rina lay on the bed and seemed to be asleep. She opened her eyes and called out weakly: "Woe, Abba has come!" It appeared to me that she shut her eyes again. For a moment, hope glimmered in my heart: "My fears had no basis, everyone in the family is fine." I asked how everyone was, and finally how Chaim was. When Chanah told me that Chaim had been wounded and taken to the hospital, and she didn't know anything about the man who had been killed in Tel Yosef, I understood that people had hidden the disaster from her.

Yehudah! Forgive me for having not yet having gotten past the first page of your work, *The Third aliyah*, which you dedicated to Chaim's memory. Nor have I as yet read your letter to me. Your dedication to your work aroused many thoughts about the life of the third *aliyah*. It is a pity that its historical account has not yet been completed.

Israel Harodi

[Page 135]

Chaim Harodi
(of blessed memory)

Israel Harodi (Solko Schmutz) was one of the first pioneers from Shomer Hatzair to make *aliyah* in the 1920s. He settled in Tel Yosef.

In 1923, Chaim was born in Ein Harod to Chanah and Israel Harodi, both of them from Zbarazh, both of them among our first pioneers. Chaim was one of the people active in defense in the area, one of the first of the new generation.

On June 29, 1946, on a "black Sabbath," a criminal hand shot him with a fatal bullet when he refused to surrender our pure weaponry to the British wretches who wanted to steal it from our hands.

———

[Page 137]

In Memory of Dear Chanah
by Yosef Blaustein

Now we have been deprived of Chanah. She was taken from her comrades before her time, leaving behind heavy pain in the hearts of her friends, acquaintances and family, a pain enveloped in many memories of her ways and her endearing relationships with others. She supported people and inspired them to hope in a proper communal type of life marked by participation and mutual responsibility.

As I stand above her fresh grave, I see the high points of her life. She was active in the pioneer movement in the city of Zbarazh in Poland where she trained, and she spent her subsequent years in the land of Israel. She came from a traditional Jewish family suffused in Zionism, which impressed its character upon her way of life. The house in which she grew up was a center of pioneer movement activities. There, the dreams of the Hakhalutz movement youth for building the homeland with a communal way of life were formed.

In 1938, Chanah made *aliyah.* In those days, there were many tensions on the Jewish street. The Polish populace, saturated with anti–Semitism, proved that there was no longer a future for the Jews in Poland. All eyes were turned hopefully toward the land of Israel, but the gates of the land were half–locked to the pioneer *aliyah.*

The pioneers sought means and ways out of the crisis. Chanah organized long discussions. She always found the proper phrase to express thoughts, yearnings and ideas, whose central axis was a fulfilled life in the land of Israel.

When she made *aliyah,* people worried for her. They wanted to help her live more easily in the city, but Chanah gently rejected their help, saying: "For my entire life, I dreamt of communal living and spoke on behalf of this type of life. Will I deny my own words and yearnings?" And the tradition of the pioneer women, which had begun in the city of Zbarazh, continued forward.

A person who brought things about and who withstood many tests, Chanah volunteered for the movement's missions, which she fulfilled with great grace and responsibility. She was well–acquainted with communal existence. Therefore, she could withstand crises. And there were such–even if no one else was aware of them.

Chanah educated her family in the spirit of the movement's values, with a motherly softness that she had received from her parents' home, but without compromises. She proved that faithfulness by half is impossible. She persuaded others of the rightness of her path, and shared her many ideas with them.

This was Chanah–a comrade, a mother, a sister–by whom we were all beautified and blessed. In the midst of her days, Chanah was taken from us–the fruit tree planted upon many waters that gave forth a blessed fruit, love and shade to all who took refuge in it.

Her memory will never be forgotten.

———

[Page 140]

Mother
by Ruti

Mother.

You were–and you still are.

And so it is hard to say anything about you. We miss your being, your ways, your soul, which had been woven into us all. Whenever I do or say anything, it appears that you will come back from some place, that you will be with us again.

To speak about you, mama? To think about you, my beloved? How is it possible? I am not resigned to the terrible truth that I will no longer see you. And how terrible this truth is.

How deeply I feel the chasm, the emptiness, the sense that I am about to be swallowed up. My world is emptied of its content. Its joy is taken from me. How will I find happiness and meaning, when you are not with me?

Why did this happen? In my deepest depths, I believed that as long as some supernal justice exists, it would not allow anything to happen to you. You so much wanted to live. You were so permeated with hope and the will for life. And you knew how to give these to everyone else, until your last moment.

I recall that bitter day, that day that will be carved in my memory forever, that time of your most difficult moments. You took us one by one, you drew us to your heart and kissed us silently in your great pain and in your terrible sufferings. That was the last time for you. You wanted to be our mother to the end–and you were. Therefore, it is so difficult to imagine the future, whatever future it might be, without you.

Mama, I want things to be good. Despite everything, I still believe that the world is fundamentally good. This too I received from you, and I try to live in accordance with these values. You knew how to live, how to find meaning in life. You knew how to love life and always see beauty and goodness in everything. That is how you were, and that is how I want to be. In my difficult moments, I will draw that strength from you—because in the depths of my heart I hear your voice calling me to live and go on.

Rest in peace, mama. And know that wherever I am, you are always with me. Your good smile, your caressing hand and the tones of your words are an indivisible part of me. We will continue on our long way, until we come to you.

Your loving daughter,

Ruti

———

To Moshe, best wishes!
by Chaveleh

I hope that you received the letter I sent you. If so, to get to the point, I have now attained the necessary material about the time when father was on the kibbutz.

And I will immediately send it to you. I hope that before the book is printed you will be able to arrange this material and incorporate it into the book, and I thank you.

Warm regards from mama!
Shalom!
Chaveleh

———

Yosef Karni

(of blessed memory)
Kiryat Anavim
by Shmuel Nardi

Yes, the row has been thinned. Another comrade has been lost and is no more. Another incidence of sudden death.

A comrade got up to go to his daily work. He walked out to the road to await the vehicle that would take him to his job in the city, but he buckled under, fell, and lay without a breath of life. He finished his work and left his life behind.

The hand of fate was very cruel, and there is no way to console and be consoled.

As we survey the 25 years that Yosef lived with us, as we pause to consider the long journey that we traveled together, we see that he was faithful to his work and to his position. He was a comrade dedicated to this kibbutz, a communal life, toward which he had been educated in his childhood in the town of Zbarazh in Galicia, experiencing a lively Zionistic life and a youth movement, in one of the towns that supplied the pioneer material that built the kibbutz movement in Israel.

Yosef dedicated himself with all his heart to this life. He was involved in everything, a comrade who did not find it hard to adapt to kibbutz work. It came to him easily. He was blessed with capable hands, and he proved his ability in everything he did.

He was lively by nature. He did not tolerate conditions that were not to his spirit. Years ago, he left this place with his family and attempted to live a private style of life, but he soon felt that his place was not there, and he quickly returned to us, to his permanent home.

Besides his main profession, Yosef tried many types of work on the kibbutz: as a driver, as a field worker in Kubaibah (when he was drafted at the height of the occurrences of 1936), as a tinsmith in a smithy that he set up with his own hands, which supplied all of the needs of the kibbutz. He was eager to see the enterprise take its place among the other enterprises that work with sand.

Recently, when he undertook the position of coordinating manufacturing activities, we all felt that he grew wings. He prepared the work and applied himself without growing weary. He spent day after day in the city and devoted his evenings to close discussions with the secretarial workers. Many plans lay before him, which he spoke of on various occasions.

We saw that Yosef was always ready to help a comrade. His ear was always turned to the request of a comrade to come to his aid as best he could.

We saw also Yosef as the head of his family, lovingly concerned for them. I often had the opportunity to hear him speak of his concern for Chanah and their precious daughters, how much effort he spent in his daughters' upbringing and education.

And we knew that only his great energy kept him going. We knew that he was plagued by illness. But Yosef did not surrender to his sufferings. He was always confident that he would overcome his pains.

As we stand at your open grave, broken and shattered, feeling no strength before the hand of cruel fate, we want to tell Chanah and her daughters that the community will do its best to help in the education and growing up of these daughters. We will try to help them so that they will be able to take their place in the community, and you will all be a living monument to his connections with this place and to the years of his life that were interrupted so cruelly.

May your soul be bound in the bond of life among the builders of our way of life.
May your memory be blessed.

————

The Wars of Israel
by Moshe Sommerstein
(Tel Aviv, 3 Shevat, 5743, 17.1.1983)

Fortunate are you, Israel, who is like you,
A nation saved by the Lord, your helping shield,
The sword of your pride. Your enemies will collapse before you,
And you will tread upon their heights.

Deuteronomy 33

In the wars of
Israel,
All of the nation's
tribes,
The entire nation of
Israel,
Battled and bled.

In the wars of
Israel,
All sons and
daughters,
All were bound
together
Around the homeland
of Israel.
Fortunate are you,
Israel...

Facing the enemy,
at the gate stood
The entire
congregation of
Jacob,
The entire walled
house,
The entire city
fortress.

Reuben at the
head of the tribe,
Simon went after
him,
Levi did not hesitate
before his foes,
Judah like a lion,
greatness is his.

Issachar from
Ta'anakh and Beth
Shean,
Zebulun from Nahalal
and Shomron,
Dan from Tzora and
Eshtaol,
Naphtali from Beit
Shemesh and Eilon.
And the children of
Joseph cared nothing
for their lives
(Ephraim and
Menashe fought on
everyone's behalf, and
on their own behalf),

The children of Gad
from the east gave
their blood,
Asher from Mivtzar
Dor, from Edom,
Fortunate are you,
Israel...

So did the children
of Jacob battle,
Against their foes,
they gave their blood,
They fought with no
concern for their
lives,
These tribes of the
nation
*Fortunate are you,
Israel...*

Generation is
linked to generation,
Back to the mighty
forefathers,
The fire of the
forefathers flickers
For the sons in public

And the enemy will
know
And will remember
this forever:
That the glowing coal
of the forefathers
Was not destined for
nothing.

The flame of the
generations
Sanctifies the blood,
The glowing coal of
the forefathers
Propels the
nation. *Fortunate are
you, Israel...*

And it will be told
from generation to
generation
How our sons fought,
how a brave and
mighty son
Overwhelmed, took
vengeance, fought and
conquered,
And crushed the
might of the foe,

For then might will
awaken anew.
The new generation
will recall the past
with praise,
It will be girded with
power, a reward
Inherited, bridging the
past to the future
Fortunate are you,
Israel...

And in the war,
"Peace of the Galilee,"
The north was in fact
Filled with anxiety
and fear,
The fainthearted and
the hawkish unified
as a nation,

The nation that
spilled its blood
Over the years
without thirst
Rose to Lebanon to
free
The nation and the
north from
degenerating

In this way, its
sons fought keenly
and faithfully
And the house of
Israel gave its blood,
The martyrs among
its sons, anew
Upon the altar of
freedom and
redemption
*Fortunate are you,
Israel...*

———

Tzvi Segal (of blessed memory)
by Moshe Sommerstein
(lawyer, chairman, Organization of Emigrants of Zbarazh and Vicinity)

He was a wonderful son of a Jewish family who dedicated all of his life to educating his family's children to lead nationalistically–informed lives. When the Zionist idea came to the town of Zbarazh, Tzvi was among the first to carry the torch of national awakening. He left the bench of learning in a Hasidic yeshiva and his pious family, and dedicated himself to the great camp of dreamers and fighters on behalf of the Zionist idea. From then on, he engaged in many deeds in the field of national work. He was a leader of the city's branch of Hitachdut Poalei Tzion, the Zionist–socialist movement. He was a teacher and educator in the Tarbut school in Zbarazh. He raised and educated a young Hebrew generation to be prepared to make *aliyah*. He got along with others, pleasant in his ways and universally beloved. It was a pleasure to speak with him. He was knowledgeable about everything, and the conversations that people had with him about participating in the city's branch of the party always left them with the impression of a fine man with pleasant ways who loves others.

He was one of the organizers of the network of Hebrew education in Volhin, and in particular in the city of Shumsk, where he educated an entire generation.

He made *aliyah* after the Holocaust, broken and shattered, after he was only able to save his daughter, Anita White. His wife, Devorah Segal, also survived. But they lost their only son, Aharon (of blessed memory), who fell during the Holocaust in 1943.

After the war, he spent time in Germany. There he was among the organizers of the socialist–Zionist Poalei Tzion movement and its Palestinian secretariat. In 1947, he was manager of the cultural division of the Central Committee of Refugees in Munchen, and that year he also participated in the first post–war Zionist Congress.

He was a straightforward, truth–speaking man who acquired the trust of all who knew him. He was modest and responsible, and pleasant to people. In particular, we people of Zbarazh felt him to be our comrade linked by bonds of friendship. With his quick gaze and warm smile, he was always open to the requests of his comrades and friends.

When he came to the land of Israel, he adapted well and he was filled with satisfaction at the fact that he was in the homeland for which he had yearned all the days of his life. Until his retirement, he worked for HaSneh, Hamerkaz, in Tel Aviv.

He always spoke about publishing the Yizkor book and said that it must be produced by the emigrants from Zbarazh. But because of his illness and his wife's difficult illness, he could not proceed with the project.

I recall how the couple gladly helped prepare for the bar mitzvah of their grandson Aaron, the son of Anita and Dr. Sidney White from the United States. There was no end to their joy.

To our great sorrow, the husband of Peninah, Dr. Sidney White (whose Hebrew name was Yishayahu ben Feivel White, of blessed memory), also passed away quickly, in April, 1982.

With the death of Tzvi and Devorah Segal, precious comrades of our flock of Zbarazh left us, but they will remain in our memories forever.

———

Moshe Hindes
(of blessed memory)
by Moshe Sommerstein

The deeds of a man are his memorial. From them, we may discern his image and his accomplishments.

He was among the first of the activists helping arouse the national movement, one of the activists of the nationalist movement and one of the builders of the Zionist socialist movement, Hapoel Hatzair (afterwards, Hitachdut Poalei Tzion), in the city.

He donated generously to Jewish national funds and recruited others to join the camp of dreamers and fighters and to make *aliyah*.

Until his last moment, he was a person of many deeds in the field of national service, a man of pleasant speech and warm to others.

He made *aliyah* after the Holocaust, when with superhuman efforts, literally risking his life, he saved two of his daughters, Marilla and Stella, who live today in Israel together with their families.

He was enthralled by the land and filled with satisfaction by seeing his children and grandchildren, and by the fact that he was living in the land for which he had yearned all the days of his life.

He was pained by the splitting of the Poalit movement in the land of Israel.

He traveled to Argentina to visit his brother Zalman. He wanted to be involved in producing the Yizkor book dedicated to the martyrs of Zbarazh, but he grew ill. He returned to the land of Israel and concealed his pains.

With his death, we lost a precious comrade with a warm Jewish heart. His name will remain carved in the memory of all of his comrades and the people of Zbarazh, who loved him.

May his memory remain forever!

[Page 157]

List of Israeli Citizens from Zbarazh and Vicinity, z"l, who died in Israel

Translated by Judy Petersen

No.	Surname	Given name	Remarks	Residence in Israel	Page
1	AHARONI	Shmuel		Zichron Yakov	157
2	BARLAS	Lina		Haifa	157
3	BRIEFER	Shmuel	Doctor	Tel Aviv	157
4	BRIEFER	Penina		Tel Aviv	157
5	BERGLAS	Menachem		Givataim	157
6	BERGLAS	Rella		Givataim	157
7	BIEBERSTEIN	Esther		Haifa	157
8	GUR	Margot		Haifa	157
9	GOLDSTEIN	Lipa		Yafo	157
10	HORNSTEIN	Tova		Ramat Gan	157
11	HINDES	Moshe		Givataim	157
12	HALPERN	Shimon		Haifa	157
13	HALPERN	Shoshana		Haifa	157
14	HALPERN	Stefa		Nes Tziona	157
15	HOLLIS	Sofia		Givataim	157
16	HINDES	Yitzchak		Or Akiva	157
17	WEINSAFT	Itamar		Tivon	157
18	WEINSAFT	Lipa		Haifa	157

19	WEINSAFT	Basha		Haifa	157
20	VIEHROICH	Klara		Haifa	157
21	WEITT	Sidney			157
22	SINGER	David		Tel Aviv	157
23	SINGER	Itamar		Tel Aviv	158
24	SEIDENORG	Gavriel		Haifa	158
25	HARODI	Yisrael		Tel Yosef	158
26	HARODI	Chaim		Tel Yosef	158
27	HARODI	Beno		Ein Shemer	158
28	TENNENBAUM	Dov		Hertzeliya	158
29	YARTZOVER	Yosef		Yafo	158
30	YARTZOVER	Chava		Ramat Gan	158
31	YAMPOLER	Meir		Tel Aviv	158
32	YULIUSBURGER	Boaz		Haifa	158
33	CARMI	Channah		Mishmerot	158
34	KATZ	Yisrael		Haifa	158
35	LANDESBERG	Risha		Tel Aviv	158
36	LANDAU	Moshe		Givataim	158
37	LANDAU	Ludwig	Doctor	Givataim	158
38	LANDAU	Ignatz		Givataim	158
39	LEVITAS	Natan		Tel Aviv	158
40	LIPA	Aryeh		Tel Yosef	158

41	LIPA	Yosef	Tel Aviv	158
42	NUSSBAUM	Leon		158
43	STROSOLER	Yehoshua	Tel Aviv	158
44	SEGAL	Devorah	Givataim	158
45	SEGAL	Tzvi	Givataim	158
46	SEGAL	Eliezer	Tel Aviv	158
47	SEGAL	Yakov	Haifa	158
48	FEDER	Leon	Ramat Gan	158
49	POLLAK	Hadassah	Givataim	158
50	PUTSCHNIK	Shalom	Kiryat Anavim	158
51	PUTSCHNIK	Yehoshua	Ramataim	158
52	FLEISCHMAN	Zalman Aharon	Tel Aviv	158
53	FELDMAN	Avraham	Rehovot	159
54	FLEISCHFARB	Moshe	Tel Aviv	159
55	KALMAN	Gusta	Petach Tikva	159
56	KARNI	Yosef	Kiryat Anavim	159
57	KRISTAL	Esther	Ramat Gan	159
58	KELLER	Moshe	Petach Tikva	159
59	KOTZEVITZKY	Fala	Kiryat Motzkin	159
60	KALISCH	Yehuda	Tira	159
61	REKER	Yakov	Petach Tikva	159

62	REKER	Esther		Petach Tikva	159
63	STERNBERG	Moshe		Bat Yam	159
64	SCHWAM	Edna		Kiryat Tel Amal	159
65	SHALIT	Shalom		Kfar Saba	159
66	SCHEIN	Yisrael		Yafo	159
67	SCHEIN	Natan		Yafo	159
68	SHAFRANSKY	Adam		Haifa	159
69	SHAFRANSKY	Shayna		Haifa	159
70	STRICKER	Tzila		Tel Aviv	159
71	SPINDEL	Yitzchak		Ramat Gan	159
72	SPEIZER	Yosef		Tel Aviv	159
73	SHERLAG	Moshe		Haifa	159
74	SPERLING	Michael		Haifa	159

Kaddish

[Mourner's prayer]

Glorified and sanctified be God's great name throughout the world which

He has created according to His will.

May He establish His kingdom in your lifetime and during your days,
and within the life of the entire House of Israel, speedily and soon;
and say, Amen.

May His great name be blessed forever and to all eternity.
Blessed and praised, glorified and exalted, extolled and honored,
adored and lauded be the name of the Holy One, blessed be He,
beyond all the blessings and hymns, praises and consolations that
are ever spoken in the world; and say, Amen.

May there be abundant peace from heaven, and life, for us
and for all Israel; and say, Amen.

He who creates peace in His celestial heights,
may He create peace for us and for all Israel;
and say, Amen.

List of Zbarazh Former Residents Living in Israel

Translated by Judy Petersen

Note: Att: Attorney, Doc: Doctor

No.	Surname	Given Name		Residence in Israel	Page
1	AVIGDORI	Rivka		Haifa	163
2	EFRON	Peppa		Tel Aviv	163
3	ASHKENAZI	Mina		Givataim	163
4	ASHKENAZI	Meir		Ramle	163
5	BAU	Rivka		Givataim	163
6	BUGAISKY	Frida		Tel Aviv	163
7	BURSTEIN	Hella		Haifa	163
8	BIEBERSTEIN	Janka		Haifa	163
9	BLAUSTEIN	Yosef		Haifa	163
10	BALIN	Yehuda		Kfar Ata	163
11	BLASS	Miriam		Ramat Gan	163
12	BARAD	Yechezkel		Tel Aviv	163
13	BERGER	Moshe		Holon	163
14	BARLAS	Chanoch	Att	Haifa	163
15	BARLAS	Regina		Haifa	163
16	GUSTMAN	Paula		Haifa	163
17	GUR	Moshe	Att	Haifa	163
18	GAZINSKY	Miriam		Nesher	163
19	GAZIT	Sarah		Kibbutz Ein Hamifratz	163
20	GRUN	Yeshai		Bnai Brak	163
21	DOVINER	Moshe		Kibbutz Mizra	163
22	DORFMAN	Sabina		Kiryat Motzkin	163
23	DARTEL	Asher		Kiryat Motzkin	163

24	DIENER	Menashe		Kfar Saba	163
25	HALPERN	Yeshayahu		Binyamina	164
26	HAMMER	Binyamin		Netanya	164
27	WAGREICH	Hertzel		Givataim	164
28	VIEHROICH	Moshe		Givataim	164
29	WEINSAFT	Avraham		Haifa	164
30	WECHSLER	Bella, Yitzchak		Haifa	164
31	HOROWITZ	Rakhel		Tel Aviv	164
32	WERBER	Klara		Tel Aviv	164
33	SOMERSTEIN	Moshe	Att	Tel Aviv	164
34	SINGER	Shifra		Hadar Yosef	164
35	SEIDENBERG	Stella		Kiryat Chaim	164
36	SELTZER	Shoshana		Givataim	164
37	ZARKOWER	Rudolf	Doc	Rehovot	164
38	TENNENBAUM	Malka		Tel Aviv	164
39	TENNENBAUM	Gatka		Holon	164
40	YULISBERGER	Tzipora		Kiryat Yam	164
41	YAKOBOVITZ	Rakhel		Haifa	164
42	COHEN	Sarah		Haifa	164
43	KAHANE	Shlomo		Haifa	164
44	KATZ	Berl		Kiryat Yam	164
45	KATZ	Yisrael		Kiryat Motzkin	164
46	CARMI	Nachman		Pardes Hanna	164
47	LIPA	Tzipora		Tel Aviv	164
48	LANDESBERG	Gershon		Ramat Hasharon	164
49	LANDESBERG	Sinai		Tel Aviv	164
50	LACKSTEIN	Gina		Tel Aviv	164
51	MICK	Shoshana		Haifa	164
52	MENDEL	Zusya		Ramat Gan	164
53	NEUHAUS	Elza		Holon	164
54	NUSSBAUM	Yisrael		Kiryat Chaim	164

55	SUSSMAN	Yisrael	Ramat Gan	165
56	STELL	Sarah	Haifa	165
57	POLLAK	Yitzchak	Holon	165
58	FEUERSTEIN	Miriam	Raanana	165
59	FINK	Ida	Holon	165
60	FISCHMAN	Truda	Tel Aviv	165
61	FELDMAN	Aharon	Rehovot	165
62	FLASCHNER	Zhenya	Givataim	165
63	FREUND	Mina	Holon	165
64	FRIEDMAN	Miriam	Ramat Gan	165
65	FURST	Aharon	Ramat Yosef, Tel Aviv	165
66	TZIMRING	Shmuel	Pardes Hanna	165
67	KIBETZ	Michael	Netanya	165
68	KLEIN	Yerachmiel	Petach Tikva	165
69	KELLER		Haifa	165
70	KELLER	Mendel	Rishon Letzion	165
71	KASIRER	Penina	Haifa	165
72	ROSENBERG	Zalman	Tel Aviv	165
73	ROTMAN	Yeshayahu	Haifa	165
74	RUNIS	David	Hadera	165
75	RAKHEL	Rivka	Hadera	165
76	RAMON	Yehoshua	Kibbutz Geva	165
77	SHVEDRON	Moshe	Haifa	165
78	STEINBERG	Avraham	Ramle	165
79	STRICKER	Yakov	Tel Aviv	165
80	STRICKER	Menachem	Tel Aviv	165
81	STERNBERG	Menachem	Bat Yam	165
82	STERNBERG	Shlomo	Bat Yam	165
83	SMUCKLER	Esther	Haifa	165
84	SHENAY	Tzvi	Petach Tikva	165
85	SPITZER	Klara	Haifa	166

86	SPERLING	Michal	Netanya	166
87	SHERLAG	Yosef	Haifa	166
88	SHERLAG	Penina	Haifa	166
89	SHERLAG	Mordechai	Haifa	166

Translated by Yocheved Klausner

As mentioned in this book, former residents of our town, those who made Aliya years ago as well as those who came after the War of Destruction, established the Organization of Former Residents of Zbarazh and Vicinity. Our mission and aim is to give a helping hand and assist those who arrive in this country and help them obtain work.

All Zbarazh people obtained work; we also acted to immortalize the holy names of our beloved, who have been sacrificed on the altar of our nation in the times of devastation in the town of Zbarazh and vicinity.

We have held yearly Memorial Services, in Tel Aviv and in Haifa, with the participation of many of our people.

In the photographs below you will see our participation in some of the memorial services. The following pages are the testimony of our activity in this respect.

Photographs

A group of former Zbarazh residents in Argentina

In the Martyrs Forest. An assembly in memory of the Poland Martyrs, with the participation of tens of Zbarazh former residents. Many of them are not alive any more.

The Martyrs Forest. Memorial assembly for the Poland martyrs. Speaker Rabbi Nurok.

Sitting: **Chairmen of the assembly Dr. Yakov Tzur and Att. Sommerstein Moshe and representatives of Poland Communities.**

The Martyrs Forest. Memorial assembly for the Poland martyrs. Speaker Dr. Yakov Tzur. Sitting: Rabbi Nurok, Att. Moshe Sommerstein et al.

Memorial assembly for the Zbarazh martyrs at the Memorial Monument, in the Zbarazh Forest.

A group of Zbarazh Jews, at Yad Vashem. Memorial service for the Zbarazh Martyrs.

A group of Zbarazh Jews, at Yad Vashem. Memorial service for the Zbarazh Martyrs.

A group of Zbarazh Jews, at the memorial service, speaker Chana Carmi.

A group of Zbarazh Jews, at the memorial service.

Memorial assembly for the Zbarzh martyrs. Speaker Louis Freungels from USA.

From right to left: **Zvi Segal, Chairman Zvi Heller, former representative in the Polish Sejm, Louis Freungels and his wife from USA, Sommerstein Moshe.**

The Yizkor Prayer

For the Soldiers of IDF

יזכור

עם ישראל את בניו ובנותיו

חיילי צבא ההגנה לישראל

הנאמנים והאמיצים אשר חרפו נפשם

במלחמות ישראל:

יזכור ישראל ויתברך בזרעו ויאבל על זיו

העלומים וחמדת הגבורה וקדושת

הרצון ומסירות הנפש אשר נספו

במערכות הכבדות:

יהיו גבורי הדרור והנצחון חתומים

בלב ישראל לדור דור.

Yizkor

The People of Israel remembers its sons and daughters devoted and brave soldiers of the Israel Defense Forces who sacrificed their lives in Israel's wars.

May Israel.......

May the heroes of freedom and victory be forever inscribed in the hearts of the Jewish people from generation to generation.

English Section

The Holocaust and the Destruction of the Jews of Zbaraz
From the Diary of an Eyewitness, the Late Yaakov Litner

I arrived ill in Zbaraz, a small town in the district of Tarnopol. I felt so bad that I doubted I'd ever recover. My legs had been wounded and I feared blood poisoning, but a miracle happened. The local Jews received us with kindness and did more for us than we could have imagined. I was put in the local Jewish hospital, and a Jewish Polish doctor operated on me. The nurses and several women doctors looked after me with extraordinary devotion. Even though the nurses wore tall mannish boots, the way they moved was incredibly graceful. In their pure white coats they seemed like winter birds that come from the cold Far East to warm the hearts of those sufferers in hospital wards such as the one where I lay in great pain.

After a while I was discharged from the hospital and as I went out into the streets, I saw a lovely town, a church, a convent, a magnificent synagogue and a castle built in the middle ages.

Here under Soviet Russian protection, I heard that Hitler had already conquered most of the world and that his armies had reached Holland, Norway, Belgium and even Paris. News of recent events reached us in very strange ways.

Somehow we tried to get by. My wife Nina and I found some food. The people of Zbaraz were very nice to us and accepted us warmly. The flames of war spread; the fire was raging and it seemed that it could not be put out... Hitler crossed the Russian border... A time of suffering lay before us.

The hell of war draws closer and danger hovers above our heads. Planes circle the town. The first bombs fell. In these moments we try to find transport but can't. Refugees flee, hungry people crowd at the shops. There is no bread, no food. The cannon fire passes over us towards the east.

We stay in our room, standing by the window and peeping out at the main street. The first grey armoured cars filled the streets and the axe and cross (Hackendreuz) flags flew overhead.

We are defeated. Towards evening it rained. The streets were filled with armoured cars and other mechanized vehicles. An old woman wandered amongst them, apparently insane, left to herself; it was hard to believe just how she had happened on this scene. This sight was illuminated from the flames of houses burning around us. Outside our door, a strange kind of traffic, soldiers walking back and forth acting decently and humanely with the population. It seems to us that these soldiers are happy to exchange a few words with us in German. The municipal egg warehouse has been requisitioned. We are forced to fry eggs for them in our stores – like an assembly line. Together with other Jews we are all made to take part in preparing their meal. These troops were from Austria and Bavaria.

The soldiers have advanced eastward. A couple of Bavarian soldiers tried to boost our spirits but after some polite words they mentioned that the S.S. were on their way. My thoughts returned to those days when I had experienced their behavior towards the Jews of Germany.

The regular army kept out of the way of the National Socialists that were on their way. The soldiers repeatedly told us "it will be bad for you". I believed them.

At the break of day, the death force started advancing. With their horns blazing, and wearing their infamous uniforms, the S.S. arrived. Intense pressure paralyzed my chest. The black trucks were like a funeral procession doing a devil's dance. A driving grey rain fell, only adding to the horrible scene.

The S.S. acted fast. The great synagogue went up in flames. Crystal Night was no longer history. Destruction, death, murder and rape came along with the bitter weather. No Jewish house was left untouched. It wasn't the end thought, the fear had just begun.

My next-door neighbor, Hindes Meir, a merchant, was forced by the S.S. to hand over the keys to his warehouse. When he answered them that the retreating Russians had the keys, the German berated him rudely. Two other S.S. men stood by, enjoying the conversation. One of them took out a gun and shot Hindes, killing him. After this "heroic act", he lit a cigarette and continued on his way as if nothing had happened.

Meir Hindes still lay outside his house. When no one was on the street, his wife ventured out for a few minutes, kneeling before her dead husband.

I saw all this through a crack in one of the closed windows. Today two Jews were sent with a wagon to take away the body. S.S. men stood looking on, ridiculing. He was buried in a plot in front of the razed synagogue. Towards evening of that same day, Meir Hindes's wife was also shot.

S.S. men chased Jews all over the city, hunting them like animals in the jungle – the jungle of Zbaraz, a small worthless settlement in the east. The houses, half of them destroyed, half still standing. We were lucky, since we lived in the center of town, opposite the Army headquarters. Probably, that is why, we remained alive.

Max Frielich who lived in the same house with us was in Tarnopol when the S.S. took over. He was among those people shot; the bullet didn't kill him but badly wounded him. He lay among the bodies with the bullet lodged in his stomach. He lay there not making a sound. During the night he awoke among the bushes, crawled through the corpses, pulling himself along till he reached the house of friends. Despite the danger, a doctor dressed his wounds and one night he was brought back to Zbaraz. Here he lay now with a high fever hidden in the cellar of our house.

The Ukrainian militia joined up with the S.S. in our city. They promised to improve our living conditions but in fact they worsened.

Now our lives depended on the S.S. on the one hand and the Ukrainian organizations on the other.

They introduced new methods of cutting off the beards of old orthodox Jews – they delighted in their deeds. The old beadle at the synagogue, a pious Jew, hung himself. Large lettered slogans proclaimed: "Only Jews have lice and lice brings disease. Stay away from Jews".

Towards evening, a car with a loudspeaker informed us that all Jews aged 15-60 were to gather in the market place at exactly 7:00 the next morning. That morning I got up very early, I got myself ready to go out, not knowing what would be expected of us, but I wanted to make a good impression. When I was just about to go out, I found the door locked. Nina, my wife, had taken the key out of the door and refused to give it to me. She had an intuitive feeling that if I were to go to the meeting in the market-place, something terrible would happen to me. Despite all my arguments to let me go, and that if I didn't, there would certainly be some unpleasantness that could be avoided, Nina refused to give in and wouldn't give me the keys.

We watched others hurrying to the marketplace from the window. A few minutes before 7:00, pandemonium broke out in the marketplace. People ran in every direction or at least tried to get away. The S.S. and the Ukrainian militia surrounded the square and pushed them inwards. Afterwards, each was asked his age and profession as if they were recruiting them for a special mission.

In the end, they were divided into two groups. In the first were those who were better dressed, representing the "intelligentsia" – and in the second group, all the others. Those in the second group were lined up to send to work; those in the first group, 72 altogether, were declared as hostages. An order was given to the Jews of Zbaraz to find – by the afternoon – 5 kilograms of tea, 5 kilograms of coffee, 150 kilograms of sugar and 200 bars of soap.

In order to free the hostages, the women and girls of the city collected all the products in baskets and by the afternoon brought them to the spot indicated, but the hostages weren't freed. The still stood in the marketplace. The S.S. arrived with trucks and the hostages were herded on – hands behind their heads, kneeling. The trucks left in the late afternoon and were never seen again.

A farmer who came to our town told us that he had heard shooting in the Lubianki forest next to the city the night they had been taken away. The next day, he had found a mass grave – freshly dug and covered.

The German administration ordered the formation of the Judenrat, apparently to assist Jews but really to be used against us. No one really knew exactly what their job was. Pinchas Greenfeld was made head of the Judenrat – a rather unpleasant man with a bad reputation. Nazism chose its own agents to carry out its edicts against the Jews.

Greenfeld, his wife and daughter, I'm sorry to say, are being given the job of fulfilling a terrible role against local Jewry. We all think, and their friends as well, that Greenfeld is willing to sacrifice everything in order to save his skin and that of his family's.

He is ready to betray Jews, to disregard everyone in order to fulfill the horrendous demands.

So that this mission might be carried out and to save the skins of the other Judenrat, Greenfeld organized a Jewish militia. Many of the town's young Jews hurried to join.

The Judenrat levied a high tax on Jews. I was forced to pay 500 zloty which is about DM 250. The funds were collected brutally. Members of the Jewish militia spared nothing and more as they went from door to door, taking anything of any value from those that wouldn't pay – wardrobes, beds, covers, bed linens. They took all this from those too poor to pay the tax levied upon them as their contribution.

[Page 9]

Since the German administration demanded that workers be found for public and other kinds of jobs the Judenrat set up an employment office. A system of bribery set in. People were afraid to leave the area, fearing to be killed or transported to a Labor Camp. They did anything to get suitable work. The Judenrat took advantage of the situation and accepted bribes and money for certain work arrangements. The sums reached 3000 zloty and more. A job next to the railway station cost more.

Jews had to hand over all leather coats, furs and woolen clothing to the Germans. Upon delivery, all items were examined. Every day, we'd read the large posters placed during the night on the walls of houses. "From today on, every Jew must wear a wide armband 10 centimeters wide on his right sleeve and on it a blue Jewish star. Those who do not abide by these orders will be punished". The next day we'd see that the armbands that one day earlier were to be worn on the right sleeve were today to be worn on the left sleeve.

The question f Jewish armbands kept the German administration very busy. We had the impression that they made these changes with the purpose of making the lives of the Jews miserable. The next morning, they again changed the order. The armband was to be worn on the right sleeve. On the streets they checked to see that the order had been carried out. Each morning, those who disregarded the order completely or did not carry out that morning's instructions, were fined 500 zloty. Today, it was decreed that anyone found not wearing the armbands would be sentenced to death.

One day, an order was given that every door and window be marked by a Jewish star on a white background – marking the houses where the Jews lived. The day was spent carrying out the order but it was not enough. The German administration demanded the notice be uniform, printed by the Judenrat with the signatures of its 3 members and the name of the apartment's owner. All this cost 100 zloty.

Non-Jews were forbidden to enter any of the marked houses. After the instructions were carried out, the Jews were stripped of their ownership and it was transferred to the government. Any one disregarding the law would be punished.

In addition to all these prohibitions, the Jews were forbidden to enter the public market but in order to stay alive, Jews had to buy food from farmers in exchange for expensive clothing or other valuables. All this under the threat of great danger. But hunger is worse than fear and there was no other choice. The farmers took advantage of the situation and demanded inflated prices. If the farmer and the Jew were caught in such a transaction, both were punished but the Jew more severely. He would be taken to the Ukrainian militia and there, beaten brutally. Notes were taken and they threatened to send the report to the German S.S. investigator in Tarnopol if the Jew didn't pay a high fine to the Ukrainian militia.

If such a report reached the investigator it meant punishment by death. The Jew would carry out the orders given by the Ukrainian Militia. The Ukrainians weren't "cruel" – they took gold, watches, rings, rugs, suitcases – anything of value. And only after their avaricious appetites had been satisfied would they destroy the report.

The Ukrainian Militia developed new large sources of income. Jews have to keep the front of their houses clean and they try to abide the order. Each morning I get up at dawn, go out and sweep the street in front of the house. The street is clean. A few hours later, a member of the militia intentionally drops a piece of paper. He comes into our house and starts to argue with me that there is a piece of paper on the street. In such a case, the fine was set at 25 to 560 zloty. Who would dare to question his decision, or do not pay the fine?

There's no branch of the Tarnopol employment office in Zbaraz. Jews must register with the office and appear in person once a week to have their work card signed. The purpose of this registration is the transport of Jews to labour.

Reports regarding the state of these camps and their methods of death were smuggled to us from those first victims who reached the camps. There was a large graveyard filled with Jewish bodies.

Today I was really in mortal danger. The secretary of the Work Office, a Ukrainian, wanted to send me to a punishment camp but one of the committee men, Vasota a meticulous but honest man, saved me from certain death. He gave me, for no payment, one of the jobs in Zbaraz. This is the same Vasota who, out of a humane attitude towards Jews, sent several Jews to work in Germany with Aryan papers which he prepared for them.

I began my new job. I work as an inspector of sanitation work in the city and am responsible for the cleanliness of the streets. Most of the workers assigned to me are old. I let them stay at home and go out by myself to do the work. I'm already up at 4 in the morning. I sweep the streets, supervise myself and am satisfied. I don't receive any wages but at least for the moment I am alive.

Day by day, the reports get worse. The sight of so many Jews in the streets angers many of the S.S. men, and Jews stay off the streets.

The father of Professor Halpern, who lives in our house, is the second chairman of the Judenrat. Tonight, the militia woke us. They demanded that Professor Halpern go to join the Judenrat, and told his father that there was a lot of work to be done preparing lists. His help was needed. This information foreshadowed the approaching danger. We dressed in order to be in a state of readiness. And when 2 hours later, we heard knocking at the door, a wave of terrible fear swept us. We frantically ran behind the house. We stood trembling in the dark. Suddenly, a light was shined in our faces. It was one of the Jewish militia men who asked us why we had run. He led us back to the house, and added that what we had done was very dangerous.

We later learned that it had been a messenger from Professor Halpern who had knocked. He had come to inform us that the "action" had begun. Even though we had known that it was coming for several weeks already – the news was a terrible shock. The horrors were approaching. We saw uniformed men with rifles patrolling the streets. Here and there we saw flashlights, and S.S. men with their white batons. They looked like devils but were worse than any of those described in books. They craved the flesh and blood of their victims. The messengers of hell of a western nation.

Yaacov Ohl lived in our house, as well as Mr. Kornberg and his wife. In the middle of the night the door was broken down. The sound of heavy boots echoed through the hall. Everyone cowered in his room, then we heard the name "Yaacov Ohl" and after it the names of Kornberg and his wife. We now knew the sound of the voice calling us to the eternal world. Our hearts pounding, we each waited to hear the next syllable, asking ourselves: Will the next name called be mine, announcing that my time has come?

At our house, they were satisfied with these 3 names and the poor souls were taken away. They left quietly and without a struggle. Similar things occurred in other houses accompanied by heart breaking scenes as families were taken away. The old man Katz told his wife when they had to join the death march: "Come, come my dear wife. We're going on our 'honeymoon'."

Terrible screams were heard from the street. At 7:30, Halpern came back. He was completely confused and crying as a result of the horrible scenes from his night with the Judenrat. The S.S. commandos demanded 530 Jews, a quota which had been filled exactly.

The S.S. wanted them brought immediately, and if one of the intended victims could not be found, another had to be sent in his place. At the Judenrat, Greenfeld had prepared an exact typed list. The victims were rounded up by the S.S. and helped by the Jewish militia.

By the early morning hours, they had been rounded up and held in the bath house. Later, they were loaded onto trucks. Three of the older men were too weak to climb on the trucks and were shot. The trucks drove off in the direction of Tarnopol.

Ohl's youngest son worked at the railroad yard at Tarnopol and knew nothing of his father's arrest. He recognized his father on the transport that passed by him. But he couldn't approach or talk to him. Father and son parted with just a glance. Both knew it was a final parting.

By now we already knew that near the city of Belz there was a center for the slaughter of Jews. It is like a factory and employs special modern methods. Transports from our district were sent there. They were used as raw materials at the plant. The clothes and the bodies of those poor souls were processed industrially – slaves as if nothing mattered. Their souls were sent upwards in a billow of smoke.

At the time of the "action", more contribution taxes were levied on us. We had to bring gold and silver articles. The Judenrat formed a committee to see that this was carried out. No one asked if he had any more to give. The evaluation was made by the confiscators, causing a great deal of distress.

A reliable source informed me that the members of the Judenrat did not participate in this contribution. Their despair took on another form. They also were not experiencing quiet nights. Members of the Jewish militia, who do not belong to the elite, are also subjects to strict guard. They must be given drink and fuel for heating.

We can hear a noise getting closer from house to house. The Nazis are demanding 250 new victims from Zbaraz. A cruel waiting period commenced once we heard about this. Greenfeld is preparing a list of deportees in the Judenrat, and as far as we have been told this list includes all the wretched and poor, whose that they regard as a burden, those that have been left completely bereft of anything that can be taken away from them.

Anyone not succeeding in hiding or not avoiding being abducted in some other way must go towards death. There was no possibility of freedom. 250 people were forcibly dragged to the bath house and imprisoned there.

They already knew what was awaiting them. Towards evening the victims were counted once more and it transpired that the full quota of deportees had not been filled; it was necessary to make up the numbers. The streets were empty. Only the members of the Judenrat and the militia, both Jews and Ukrainians, were to be seen in the streets. Suddenly out of the silence around, could be heard the sounds of wailing and sighing. A couple had been kidnapped and transported. The husband was carrying in his hand a package all wrapped up – his 3 year old son – and all the way he was stroking him. His wife was crying and held on to the arm of her husband. My heart broke to hear these cries. I saw the wretched people and there was nothing I could do to help them. At any moment the same fate could have overtaken me.

In our house there were still 23 Jews before the 'action' that was about to befall us. Each one of us was racking his brains to find some solution – some way out. We conducted joint discussions, but to no end. We are trapped animals. More than once it had occurred to me that it would be better just to lie down and not get up anymore. Afterwards I overcome these feelings, and I feel inside me that God will save me.

In the end we agreed all of us together, to build a secret bunker; we chose for this purpose a dark room in the corridor. We blocked up the entrance, and nobody could have known that this place hid an empty chamber behind it. Working very hard, we drilled a hole from our apartment that led to the hiding place, and we camouflaged this with much imagination. From the day that the 'actions' began, we established a special night duty. This duty exhausted our strength but the morale and fear gave us the strength to carry on.

Sometimes there's a false alarm. The guards heard some sound and then we all entered the secret bunker. We knew that such an eventuality was possible, and that we would have to spend a long time in this dark, damp room. There were also children amongst us, and coughing, rasping, and carrying could have meant the end for all of us.

Younk Ohl was dismissed from his work at the railways and was accepted into the militia. Sometimes he would work on the night duty and then he would know of any approaching danger. His young wife, Tonia, her parents and the young daughter Naomi were with us in the bunker. For this reason, Ohl's interest was even greater, and he was careful to warn us in time. This gave us a certain amount of security. The bunker was terribly narrow. Many of the people snored in their sleep because of the damp and the lack of air. We were forced to wake them up because their snoring could have given us away.

One night Ohl was all ready for the midnight shift and I was on guard duty at our bunker. Opposite our house was the station of the Ukraine militia. And then, in the middle of the night, a car arrived and somebody asked in German: "Where is the Judenrat?" I looked out very carefully, and saw S.S. men sitting in the car wearing their white coats. I felt fear choking me. The situation was very serious; Ohl and I woke up the others in order to get them immediately to the bunker, and Ohl carefully closed the hiding place and made his way to the Judenrat. Before that we had spread all the personal belongings and furniture around the flat and opened the door in order to give the impression that the actions had already passed by here. After a few minutes, Ohl returned from the Judenrat and warned us from the other side of the wall that we have to be particularly quiet. It seemed that a very comprehensive witch-hunt was in progress. How can I describe in writing our situation in our little hole? That particular day I was feeling weak. The air was choking and time seemed to stand still. Suddenly we heard the sound of steps. They came nearer and nearer and then they were in our apartment. Silence! We held our breaths in order that our hearts shouldn't beat too loudly. These were moments of decision that could mean life or death for us. The Germans spent a long time in our apartment; afterwards we felt that the search as over. We breathed a sigh of relief. The footsteps left. The pressure subsided slowly but we still had to be very careful. The lack of oxygen in our hiding place was more and more apparent. We sat with our heads down, breathing heavily. Ohl only arrived the next afternoon, after we had waiting for him eagerly. We were happy to leave our hiding place that had saved us from death. Ohl explained why he hadn't come to release us earlier. The action had continued right through the second day into the early hours in the most frightening way. Men, women, children and old people – they did not leave out a single house. That day we felt paralyzed; again we heard of acquaintances who had been visited by the terrible fate of death, and Zbaraz had supplied over a thousand people to the extermination machine.

One of Zbaraz's citizens, a dentist, managed to escape from the transport of those sent to death, and he related: "At six in the morning I was kidnapped by the police next to my house, I was wearing my slippers, and one of the army men said: 'Look, you haven't even got shoes on!' The other one answered: 'If he's going to his death, he doesn't need any'. All those kidnapped in our district were gathered at the public square, and for some unknown reason we had to kneel down. After a lot of pain and fear, we were transferred in groups to the bath house; the place was full of other kidnapped people. They pushed us inside forcibly and beat us with rubber batons. Cries filled the air. Children choked and some people were already standing on the corpses of others. We were there for 2 hours.

"Afterwards they took us out from there and took us 2 kilometers towards the railway. They forced us to sit crossed legged with our heads held backwards. This was the order that the sadists gave in order to fulfill their quota of cruelty.

"Here they hit us again. One of them in uniform stood guard over the wretched brigade. At first we were told that we had to lift our hand if we needed to excuse ourselves. Then the S.S. man was heard to yell 'What? To the toilet? No! Do it in your pants like at home!' In this wretched state, worse off than a flock of sheep, we remained until the evening. Afterwards they counted the flock. All the men between the ages of 16 and 40 were stood in special lines and sent to the work camps, most of them to the town of Lemberg. The rest were sentenced to death by a thumb sign of the S.S. leaders.

Those that had been sentenced to death were pushed into closed wagons and sent to the crematoriums and extermination camps in Poland. The wagons were sealed up. The whole of the yard in front of the railway was lit up with projectors and armed guards stood round the wagons. Twice I fainted. I wasn't the only one. The wagons had no windows, the sole air vent was closed up from outside. At about 9:00 in the evening the train left. My heart was informing me that my chest was about to explode. I yelled and yelled together with my father who was with me in the same wagon. His sole concern was for our mother. If she had been with us we would have willingly gone together to our deaths. And then I thought of escaping. We weren't scared of trying, because we knew that our fate had already been sealed. One of us had a large knife. I started to saw the plank that was blocking the window until the opening was bigger. What men are capable of doing in such situations! My father and I were ready for it. The train slowed its journey for a few minutes and I jumped out. My father jumped after me. We were both injured a little but we did not feel the pain.

We ran back on foot to Zbaraz. I was still wearing my slippers and my feet were completely bloody. Others also managed to escape from that wagon, but some of them paid with their lives. They were crushed to death mercilessly by the wheels of the train. The same fate they would have received from the Germans or the Ukrainian murderers.

It was decided to establish a ghetto. The order was given that the Jews had to go and live in the same part of the town that had previously been the horse market.

This is where all the municipal garbage was brought, and we were obviously considered as garbage. In summer the place is full of flies and biting mosquitoes; the stench was terrible like in hell. The move to the ghetto had to be completed within 24 hours. The Jews of Podvoloziska were also transferred here. The small number of houses was not enough for all of them and could not hold everyone. We are going to have to make do with 20 people to a room. Many people have to sell their furniture or to exchange it for other goods. It's interesting that the local farmers, well-known for their avarice, very quickly got used to the new situation. Already in the early hours of the day, they were standing in lines in front of the Jewish quarters waiting for the right moment to rob them of their belongings. The ghetto looked like a complete disaster area. The filth and the despicable behavior of the farmers carrying off the good only added to the disgust. Broken furniture stood in front of the houses; and horse droppings were everywhere. Here again I was put in charge of cleaning the street, and I carried this work out with a broom like Hercules – with no results.

This was an unsuccessful war. Until that period, I had never seen so much wrong. Farmers took all the furniture that we couldn't take into our new houses. "You should be happy", they taunted us "that we're giving you something in return. In any case, you don't have much time left to live". The mood in the ghetto reached rock bottom. Peoples' faces showed their despair. Some of them had already accepted the idea that their life had come to an end, and all that they wished for was that the end would come as fast as possible. Others who still had a little spark of the desire to live in them, was living in perpetual fear. These were all broken people, who knew that they faced a terrible and unavoidable end.

The Jewish militia was increased in size from 80 to 130 men, a sure sign that a new action was being planned for us. Greenfeld knows for certain what has to happen. The Jews are so scared of him as of the S.S. hangman. He is convinced that by betraying his friends he will save his family. The members of the militia hold onto their posts in order to ensure their lives. These men pay astronomical sums, up to 10,000 zloty in order to become member of the militia. I once read in a book about a ship that sunk and on the fight for survival that these men fought in order to save themselves. Everything is in a state of destruction in the ghetto. Life is cruel and the people are cruel. How many guards there are over us – the Jewish militia, the Ukrainian militia, the regular S.S., the special S.S., t he S.S. gendarmerie, S.S. police – all of them guarding us in our wretched ghetto.

Often inspections were made for food items. If food was found in the ghetto, it was thrown into the streets. I sweep up a lot of such food items. I was even capable of eating it, so hungry was I. The Germans and the Ukrainians want to know how stocked up the Jewish houses are, and woe unto him who's house was found to contain more than the right amount of food stuffs. These inspections are the best opportunities for blackmail of every kind.

There is a wedding today at the Judenrat. One militia man is marrying the daughter of Greenfeld, the head of the Judenrat. For us the regular Jews, the meaning of this celebration was an emergency tax.

The Jewish identity cards were returned to the security service in Tarnopol for reexamination. They had to have the stamp of the security services, otherwise they would not be valid; for anybody found without one, life was not worth living.

Greenfeld travelled to Tarnopol to get the cards stamped, our lives were again terribly threatened. Our fear was that Greenfeld would foul things up. Our future depended on these cars being stamped. Does Greenfeld himself know when he is going to bring these cards back? Greenfeld returned from Tarnopol saying that he only brought some of the card back stamped. The stamp costs a great deal. I myself had to pay 1,000 wretched zloty for my own card – and all that for maybe a few more days of life. We are completely obsessed with getting our stamped cards as if it was the only medicine that prevented us from the death sentence. The tragedy of the commerce in stamps continues.

Many of those who worked in the brick factory of the Eastern railway or the railway track did not receive their cards and were in despair at the astronomical sums that they had to pay for the stamp.

Greenfeld travelled again to Tarnopol. A wild and filthy trade began over our lives. Man no longer exists – only the stamp.

All of the inhabitants of town of Viznovich fell victim to riots. One doctor with his wife and child were able to escape. Brininger, a long time apostate, brought the doctor and his family to his home and gave them shelter. However a neighbor reported him, and he and his family and all those that he had given shelter to were taken to Tarnopol and were all shot.

Fear of a new action is growing daily. We no longer dare to undress at night. Every house has a guard whose job is to see what's going on in the streets. They're building bunkers everywhere in order to hide. When people see death before their eyes, they bury themselves like moles in the ground. The building of our bunker was particularly difficult because our house was on a hill; there was no cellar and the whole thing was likely to collapse. We dug out from the floor a hole just large enough for one person to get in. This hole was covered with a mud plank. So successfully that when it was closed, nobody could guess that there was a hidden entrance there.

The tunnel began here. We did this work with the simplest tools and with plates. We worked very hard, scratching he dirt and plaster. Panic pushed us to work faster. Every moment and every hour was very important for us. We worked with all our might at night without any light. Sweeping up the earth caused us many problems. We would take out the earth and cover it up with snow and frozen ground. We had to be very careful because the militia men who guarded the ghetto examined – with the help of torches – everyone who went out at night and woe betide anyone who got caught. Finally four people managed to squeeze into our bunker. In order that we might be able to sit down, we filled some sacks with earth and place the planks on them. Inventory of the bunker included a pot for excusing ourselves, candles, and a thermos with drinking water.

We Jews were particularly frightened of the 9th of November. The night arrived. We were all awake and ready for anything that might transpire. At midnight Ohl knocked on the window and whispered that the action had begun. Like frightened mice we scrambled into our hiding place. The situation inside was indescribable. Four men waiting with their hearts beating for the danger of death to recede. The passage was very narrow. We had difficulty breathing. Suddenly we heard voices and heavy footsteps above us. They were here. We stopped breathing. Again these were minutes that were determining our fate. And then we heard cries; "Jews, out!" They knocked with their rifles on the floor to search for hiding places and tunnels. Time stood still. Death was looking for us. The knocking of the rifles was like the knocking f our own bones. We were covered in dust, and at any minute they could have found us. At last there was silence. We were given our lives back again. We very carefully let air into our hiding place, but we were still scared to leave. We only left the following day. We looked terrible. Our clothes were full of plaster and dust; we were thoroughly drenched inside and out, because the conditions of the lace did not allow us to excuse ourselves. We came out like shadows arising from the underworld. The tragedy is immense, but we are all alive. The despair in the streets is even greater, where fathers, mothers, children, husbands and wives are searching for one another. The heart rending cries are terrifying. Some are shouting, others are tearing their clothes.

Some are walking around in despair, in silence, with a fixed stare. Hunger is driving them to robbery and theft in the streets. I saw a young child with a loaf of bread under his arms; a short man is struggling with various household items; thieves get in through the windows in broad daylight. The houses are deserted – the residents have left never to return.

Later, we learn from the farmers of the shocking total of 1,050 victims that were taken that night. Slowly but surely the houses of the people that left were closed and locked up. The Jewish militia was given this task, but before they were allowed to start, official permission was given to loot the Jewish property. From Tarnopol, there arrived a unit of the S.S. commando, headed by some bishop, a very special person. He arrived accompanied by his mistress Yedvika Pertika from the German nationalist movement. With the help of his gun and his baton he personally took part in this robbery. He was accompanied by two militia men. One of them was Greenberg, the brother of the other "Oberman". Greenberg held a bottle of Vodka in his hand for the bishop. When the bishop reached the place, he left all his followers outside. To the question "how come you haven't yet been transported?", I said "I work". The bishop demanded to see my identification and check it very carefully. He ordered me to empty my pockets. All this time he was waving his baton in front of my face, threatening to hit me several times. Afterwards he stole my wallet from me, and my silver watch, a pen and stamps; he also removed from my finger the little gold ring that I received from my late mother.

I was forced to carry on working in the street, clearing the way for our oppressors. I soon developed pneumonia, due to the lack of clothing and insufficient food. The rats crawled over my bed fearlessly, and paid me a sick visit. The people who came to visit me weren't laughing. Shmajuk was here today. His parents, his sister and his wife had been put to death. Igor Greenberg sat by my bed yesterday. He is one of the few that were released from the punishment camp. At home he found his wife and children, but his brother, sister and brother-in-law had been killed. I had very sleepless nights.

The Judenrat distributed alcohol to members of the Jewish militia. The rumor spread like a flame in the ghetto. We knew what this meant – a new witch-hunt was about to begin.

I'm still ill, and even so I'm forced to go down to the bunker. In a state of complete collapse. I bent down in order to get into the damp hole. To our misfortune, when the sign was given to start the big witch hunt, two strangers were with us. In the confusion they were also shoved down into our bunker, even though there really wasn't room for them. I was so cramped that we asked the strangers to leave, and to allow us to get into the bunker. They left and ran off. There was silence in our bunker. We hear the voices of militia men. They spent some time in the room, and left again. If we thought that the danger had passed, however, we were mistaken. At about 5:00 in the morning, other militia men came. They went straight toward our hiding place, removed the partition of the hiding place, and knocked. This was a result of treachery by somebody against us, genuine treachery. We had to remove the partition at the opening, and we all left trembling. I alone remained inside lying down. They took my son Mietek; but they couldn't take me because of my illness. My wife Nana ran back and forth in complete despair because of our only son that they had taken, and afterwards she ran to the Judenrat to try and release him. I remained alone, in despair, powerless, in my "grave". My temperature rose, and I started to imagine that I was buried alive. The opening to the hiding place was very narrow, like the neck of a bottle. It seemed that I had been pushed through the neck of the bottle inside, and the cork had been placed on it. I asked myself how I would ever be able to regain my strength in these circumstances.

I felt as if I were shot from above and below and in this way I had been finished off. My despair was so great that I prayed for a bullet to once and for all end my misery. Suddenly five militia men arrived. They dragged me out and roughly forced me to leave through the narrow opening. They threw me on the floor of the apartment, and I lay there groaning. I was overcome by giddiness and I felt as if I was in a stationary car, with its engine on and everything shaking.

It seems that my condition aroused the mercy of the militia men. They didn't do me any harm, and sent to call a doctor. Another miracle occurred. My son Mietek was released in the Judenrat, and my wife Nina was very happy. We were able once more to think about continuing our struggle to live.

At five o'clock in the morning I awoke to the sound of wild shooting. I jumped out of bed and looked out the window. Men in uniform were disturbing the morning serenity. Others, not in uniform, were firing their guns in all directions. I woke all the others up immediately. They hadn't heard the shooting. We were in despair. We could not get dressed. All around the house we heard terrible shouting. We grabbed our clothes and again we squeezed into our hiding place in the bunker. In the excitement, I forgot to take my shoes with me and I found myself barefoot on the Damp cold ground. We were all trembling. We were not allowed to move. Outside, death was all around us and the shots did not cease. The hunter could reach our room at any moment All around we heard terrible cries that froze our hearts as if an icy finger had touched us My throat was dry, my pulse was racing, my forehead was filled with cold sweat. This was an awful hour spent in fear of death.

This time we were certain that the end had come. Then all of a sudden a miracle occurred. The angel of death passed us by and went on. The hunter departed, and the shouts, yells, and shots vanished as if they had never been at all. At daybreak, Mietek decided to leave the bunker and Nina went out after him. He thought that he should go to the Judenrat. He managed to prepare bread and water for us, threw me my shoes, and left the house. We sat waiting in our dark tunnel. An hour later, Mietek returned to our apartment and warned us that a very widespread action was in process. Until now, he said, 900 Jews had already been rounded up. Our anxiety increased. About lunchtime, Mietek returned again. He was in great despair, his fiancée was rounded up and he wished to free her. In previous actions the militia men had managed, with great effort, to free people close to them. They had to go to the head of the SS actions and to say "I have worked very well". Cohanic, one of the militia men, managed in this way to free his parents, but in return he had to bring in 24 other Jews.

He wished in this way to release his sister also, but he didn't manage, since he was unable to round up another 12 Jews. At half past four in the afternoon Mietek returned once more. We were still sitting frozen, statue-like in our bunker. Mietek said that his fiancée had been released but had been transferred meanwhile to the railway station and that he was hurrying there. Several hours passed, hour after hour, and Mietek did not return.

It was a very long night. We spent the whole night in the bunker. Eventually after 24 hours in the bunker, we left our hiding place at 6:00 in the morning. I dared to go out into the street. The dead were again lying at the side of the road. Their limbs were frozen. Their blood had colored the snow. Some of the Jews that still remained dared to go out into the street, stealing furtive glances at each other, like hunted animals. We then discovered that Sternberg, the commander of the Jewish militia, together with 48 militia men, had been shot to death. 1,050 Jews had been shot by the militia. Militia men buried them, and then they themselves stood in front of the firing line and they were all cut down.

My wife Nina's feeling that our son Mietek was one of the tragic victims turned out to be true. The ghetto was like a city of death. The tense quietness of the empty streets had a terrible effect on us. The empty houses looked like a ghost town, with their empty windows and opened doors. Eyewitnesses reported that the victims of that terrible day were under tight guard on the empty yard in front of the bath house, and the "animals" ordered them to get down on the damp ground.

When they realized that they were going to be searched, some of the victims buried those valuables that they still possessed in the ground underneath them. The ground was frozen, and they dug with their fingernails until they were completely bloody. Afterwards they were taken in groups to the bath house, where they were undressed, and forced to walk 3 kilometers through the town, completely naked. They were shot in groups of 20. The next day all the documents and photographs of the dead were still in the bath house.

The wind, together with a few children, was playing with them. One of the children was holding a photograph of a good friend of mine. At my request the child gave me the photograph.

Today the order was given to go through the clothes of the dead. Their rings and all other valuables and jewelry were gathered together in bags. Only 900 people still remained in the ghetto. None of them with any hope of being saved. We are a city doomed to be lost. Informed sources tell us that Zbaraz will be completely free of Jews by the end of this month.

Children playing in the yard by the bath house found some of the jewelry belonging to the victims. Looters came from far and wide to dig up the ground and take the gold of the miserable people who had left it there – they found jewelry, gold, silver, and dollar notes. This was a very sad looting. The remainder of the militia men no longer wished to serve their masters, and threw away their special armbands. There are now vacancies in the militia for no payment. A new Judenrat has been organized and at the beginning of its term of office it faces financial problems. It therefore proposes to impose an emergency tax.

I have never been so depressed. My hands shake. I cry without stopping. I feel like a little neglected child. I am no longer human. Today I went out with a few other men to prepare a mass grave for the dead. This mass grave was covered with a thin layer of earth, and blood was still all around. A terrible stench rose from the pile of bodies. Jackals were scratching the ground, and would take away with them limbs from the dead.

A farmer's dog brought home the hand of one of the victims. Every day some of the men had to go out to cover the grave again. There is no way of describing how terrible this work was. Miss H, a beautiful 18 year old girl, was told by the S.S.: "You really are very beautiful, that's why we'll give you two bullets". A 22 year old woman, who had not been killed by the bullets, rolled on the ground screaming that she wanted to die. "Why do you want to die", asked the S.S. man "Jews don't die, they just rot away". A five year old boy opened his eyes wide at the murderer. "Yes my little one, I even have a bullet for you", the German said to him. It looks as though Zbaraz is going to be entirely rid of Jews, and we have to do something to try to save ourselves.

We have started to negotiate with a Ukrainian farmer, and he has promised to give us a place to sleep, naturally in exchange for hard cash. Today he took us in his cart with the beds, bedclothes, clothing, linen and a little food. We gave him 300 zloty as a down payment, and we think that this give us a good chance of getting out of this place. We did not imagine that anybody would wish to help us.

This is how the evil started. The punishment for leaving the ghetto was death. But we had to escape. We had been condemned to death in any case. This was our only chance. We waited until twilight, and we decided to leave the ghetto. When we reached the last house of the ghetto, we removed the symbol of our Jewishness, our armbands. We hid. We were not afraid of the Jewish militia, who themselves were wandering around the forest. We made our way like something out of a story about Red Indians, but far more dangerous. I felt very unwell. I could only move very slowly, making my way along the paths through the fields. A few times I almost gave up.

The moon was hidden as if it wished to disappear from the night. We held each other's hands so as not to get lost in the fields. A dog barked. We were very frightened. Every minute could have taken us out of that night. Finally, after much effort, we reached the farmer's yard. I collapsed under a tree. I was at the end of my strength, but I felt that I had been saved. The farmer moved us to a barn, and laid us down on the straw. It was very cold. At dawn the farmer's son came and frightened us. Some committee, he said, has to come and check the place over, and we can't stay here. The son was very unfriendly, even hostile. He opened the barn doors since he wanted us to get out of there fast. We did not dare to make for open ground. We couldn't decide what to do, because we felt that we could not leave our hiding place. Another hour of anxiety passed over us. Then the farmer came, and he was extremely worried. He was worried and very angry because his children were not agreeing to our staying there. We felt sorry for him and for the trouble he was being caused by his children. "It's not nice of them", he told us. "We will have to think of building you a bunker". In the meantime his wife came and brought us a pail of hot milk and a bowl of boiled potatoes. We were very hungry and devoured the food. The farmer's wife looked at us if we were animals, the way we behaved.

When we finished eating, she told us that we would have to leave their yard. She was scared for her family. In the mean time all was quiet in Zbaraz, she said. All our pleas were to no avail, we had to leave. We were desperate, and did not know how to start all over again. We were very anxious at the prospect of returning. We remained there lying down and after a few minutes a young blonde girl came to the barn and started screaming with fright when she saw us. Then we heard shouts of people in the yard. Now we had no choice but to escape from the place.

We ran like blind men through the fields. We coughed and groaned from the fear that gripped us. At this time of year, it was already quite warm during the day. Farmers working in the fields paid no attention to us. Spring had started. We ran back into the trap, back to the ghetto, to the hiding place, to death. After the difficulties of our escape, we now retraced our steps like snails. On the main road, I suddenly felt breathless. I sat down and could no longer get up again. Had my final hour arrived, death, redemption? From a distance I saw a farmer, who almost ran us over. I felt bad, and in no way could I look after myself. Nina prayed, she was completely bewildered. She begged, out of her despair: "O fate, o fate! You have to walk" she said to me. But I couldn't. I remained seated helplessly. The farmer was by our side in an instant. "Where's your arm band?" He asked in Ukrainian. Nina answered him in Polish but he realized that we were Jews who had fled from the ghetto. He insisted that we go with him immediately to the militia. With inhuman pain, I managed to drive myself a little forward and then fell down again. I went down on my knees, and begged him to save us. I asked him what benefit he would derive if they kill us. The farmer thought a little, and brought us to a little grove by the side of the road. There was nothing we could do, and we carried on crawling out of that place. We were lost. At the best, a bullet awaited us. With the fear of death over me, I stroked the farmer's face to try and influence him to change his mood towards us.

After he examined my purse and that of Nina, he took from us 360 zloty, the last of the money that we possessed. I had to undress and I stood there naked in front of him. He searched all my clothes, feeling around everywhere, to no avail. I did not have any more money. In the end, he kicked me, and silently turned away from us. He went away and we had been saved once more. We walked farther without meeting anybody until we got back to the ghetto. As we ran back into the ghetto, we passed a hut from which we heard joyous voices, singing and loud laughter. We did not understand what the gaiety was about. In such a miserable situation, in an atmosphere of prey, such joyous voices sounded like a ghost's dance. This laughter and singing caused us terrible mental anguish, and although we were terribly tired, we could not take one step further. We looked into the hut and what did we see? Inside the hut sat young Jews who were singing and overflowing with freedom. We realized that they refused to accept their fate in life, and had decided to flee into the forest.

Our house was empty. The farmer had taken all our belongings when we went to the hiding place that he promised us. A hatbox and a small suitcase was all that was left in the house. The ghetto had become smaller and other groups had reached us. The few remaining Jews had been given houses next to the bath house.

We had to leave our house within 24 hours, and there was not yet room for us by the bath house. That day was my birthday. I tried to find a new place of refuge in the area, but by the end of the day I had no roof over my head and we decided to stay another night in our old place and to sleep on the floor. This was the night of ghosts. Not only was there no light in the ghetto, but everything seemed dead. In the middle of the night we heard knocking. These were the people who had come to loot the houses of the dead. As the moon rose, they went like mice from house to house. We knelt down full of fear on the bare ground. Suddenly the door of our room burst open. In the doorway we saw the shadow of a man illuminating us with his torch. His lighted cigarette end could have betrayed us, as he stood there by the door. We held our breaths. It was like a dream. We waited for something to happen any second. What would be with this man? After a minute he disappeared, with the small light of his cigarette receding into the darkness. The door was slammed. He had left.

Professor Halpern Munio took pity on us, and took us into his little room. He was there with his wife and small son and another child whose parents had been killed during the last 'action', whom he had adopted for himself. We could only lie down in a corner of the room, but at least we had a roof over head, and shelter from the militia guards that were chasing us in the street.

The remnants of the ghetto looked like an underground cell. Jews met each other in the streets as if they had been resurrected from the dead. They greeted each other without words, the greeting accompanied by tears. We look like fish in the fish shop with our number getting steadily less. In the morning, S.S. men came twice to the street of the Jews, and each time there was a commotion. The potato soup of the Halpern family was passed from hand to hand in the darkness. After the meal, I sat down to write and Nina was busy with the dishes. Halpern's wife got herself ready, changed her linen, and put on her expensive dress. After that she asked me to read to her husband and son. While I read to them, she spoke quietly with my wife Nina. Nina was very perturbed. Mrs. Halpern told her husband and son that she asked for their forgiveness, but she had to leave now. She stretched her hand out to me and said, "I must say goodbye to you now". Tears choked us. Professor Halpern was unable to restrain himself. The child cried instinctively from fear. I cried out anxiously "No you can't do this!", but it was already too late. She took poison. She fell unconscious on the couch, and she died towards morning after having poisoned herself with luminal. A ghetto resident could not call a doctor. She had rid herself of the sorrows of this life. Many Jews had prepared poison for themselves.The young men that we had met in the hut, whose singing we heard when we returned to the ghetto, fled to the woods. They wanted to find their way to Valin and to join the Partisans there. They never managed. The same day that they escaped to the forest no far from Zbaraz, murderers fell upon them and killed them.

One of them was brought in a critical condition to the Judenrat, and died a few hours later. Now we were in their hut.

Something else was also happening. Children were playing on the street of the Jews, Jewish children. We saw them through the window playing at "actions". They built themselves hiding places and bunkers, they hid in them, and afterwards pretending to be S.S. men, they came out of the bunkers and chased everybody away, pointing wooden guns at them to kill them. This game frightened me, because I saw before me the game of the future, and their fate.

Large posters were put up in the town of Zbaraz and surrounding villages: "Anyone giving shelter to Jews will be put to death".

Early next morning we head unrelenting shooting from the direction of the ghetto. Sometime later, the baker came and told us that the action was progressing furiously. He told us that many of our friends had poisoned themselves at home and in the streets. Others had been shot. They were forced to dig their own graves, and afterwards they stood next to the graves and were shot. The hammer of machine gun fire was heard right through the night. Then there was silence. Death had its fill. The last 'action' was over. The S.S. men worked thoroughly. The town of Zbaraz was finally completely free of Jews.

We laid down like blind men in the darkness. We learned to move like blind men. There had been a terrible noise in the ghetto. It was difficult for us to get used to the quiet in our new place. The cement walls allowed no sounds to get through to us from the outside world; we were closed in with our sighs and with our fear.

Slowly but surely we became completely silent. We were frightened of our own voices. Nina and I developed an ability to understand each other without words.

There was a terrible winter at this time. We laid down frozen together, clutching each other like animals in the den. The walls of our hiding-place are no longer damp, they are covered with frost. When our landlord came to us, to the other part of the hut, he brought with him snow. It seems that we were making a bad impression on him. We were full of mould. The mould and the frost got through to our clothes and penetrated to our skin. Our eyesight was weak. We were scared that we would go blind. The baker told us today that the Red Army is progressing, and that the Germans are retreating. Will the Bolsheviks save us? Will they find us alive? We have no more food left, and both the landlord, and the baker are demanding money from us. I was wondering what one can do when there is nothing more you can do to help yourself. In my misery I suddenly remembered the gold bridge that capped my teeth. But how was I going to remove this from my jaw? For that you need a dentist, which was out of the question. I chose to do it myself, and I took a long time. These were terrible hours of pain. My teeth and my jaw hurt, my gums bled, and I developed a fever. At last I managed to take out my good tooth, on which the gold bridge was beginning to wobble. I took courage, and separated the tooth from the bridge. I gave the gold to the landlord so that he could sell it to a dentist. He told me that he received 3,500 zloty for the bridge. I gave him half, and part of the money went to the baker. We thus received another respite. We had quiet, and bread, for a little while longer. The baker started giving us better food. He told us that the Germans were preparing defense positions, and all the signs pointed towards a terrible defeat for the German army. This was our hope.

It looks as though the German army wants to defend the town of Zbaraz. From today in the afternoon, we've been hearing the sounds of cars in the direction of Tarnopol, in other words to the west. It seems that they really are contemplating retreat. After that, the machine guns ceased. In our bunker we felt an earthquake from the cannon fire. We were like in fever. Our bodies trembled, our hands are almost paralyzed. It looks as if freedom is not too far away.

We are free! The miracle occurred and the hour of our redemption has arrived. The moment that we have been waiting for has finally come to pass. Our landlord arrived and told us that the Russians are approaching the city. Then came the baker and told us that he has seen with his own eyes the market place full of big tanks. We were so happy that we could not express a word. Freedom is near. We could not utter cries of joy but mumblings of confusion. We did not dare to go out to our freedom. We also had no strength to leave our hole. Furthermore, the landlord, for reasons that we could not fathom, was still afraid to let us out of the bunker. He was hoping to put the Russians up, but did not inform them of our being there.

We were terribly nervous, and we spoke louder and louder. Our voices were heard above. Three Russian officers came down to the cellar, with their guns cocked to see who was hiding there.

We called them and told them who we were. The officers came down to us and we showed them our personal papers that we still had with us. The Russians were moved at our story. They found our photographs and did not believe that we were the same people: we had become burrowers, and I believe that the Russian officers were inclined to keep us that way.

We could hardly move our limbs, and were too weak to go outside. They had to bring some Red Army soldiers to take us out of our hole. After so many months, I saw the sun again. It stood there colored reddish beige, above the snowy landscape.

The combination of the cellar, freedom, the sun, and the snow, put us into turmoil. We fell to the ground. We were like people reborn, barely able to move properly in this world. We had to learn to walk again, to move again, and this took 4 weeks. We slept with closed eyes. Were we in paradise? The Russians put a guard over us. Officers and regular soldiers guarded us, each one of them making certain to bring us some sort of present, or to help us in some sort of way. The terribly dark night had passed, but the war was still on. We had experienced a miracle.

Today we made our way past the old ghetto. It was a terrible and painful experience. Only a few houses remained of those that had held more than 5,000 Jews. The others were completely destroyed. With great difficulty I managed to find some of the houses where I stayed during that terrible period. In the street, I walked on the same pavements that I had swept earlier. I saw parts of gravestones from the Jewish cemetery spread all over the streets of the town. Hebrew lettering could still be read on the broken tombstones. In the children's home today, they showed me a Jewish child who somehow had been saved from death. During the disturbances at the time of the 'actions' against the Jews, a farmer's wife in the area brought the murderers a Jewish 3-year-old child who had been given to her, so that she should save him from the murderers. The woman gave the child to an S.S. man, and told him that she did not want to hide him anymore. The S.S. man sat him in the yard of the burnt out synagogue. The child sat there, not knowing what was happening. A shot was heard in the direction of the child, but the bullet missed and the child laughed at the murderer. The latter reloaded, but the second bullet also missed the child. The same happened with the third. Worried, he turned to a Ukrainian militia man and ordered him to take the "Jewish skin" to be baptized in the church. I heard this story from a living witness from the town of Zbaraz. He assured me that this is what happened. Many people were no trying to take this child under their wings.

Today the Russians started excavating and bringing up the victims of the 5th and 6th "actions". An investigating committee arrived from Moscow and from other towns, in order to establish on the spot the facts of the mass murders. Most of the Zbaraz population, doctors, soldiers from the Red Army, and all those that remained out of the 5,000 Jewish victims, went with the investigating committee to the burial site, the local petrol station, "Neftostroy". For many of the Jews who had just come out of hiding, this was an opportunity to meet up again with their colleagues in similar circumstances.

Each one had suffered his own fate. Each one had his own problems. The look of death stared from the eyes of all. One told the other of the terrible tragic circumstances that had overcome him, and each case of escape was a miracle.

We gathered here by the grave of the victims for a memorial. It was a terrible sight. The head of the investigating committee, some Russian major, gave a speech. After that 30 young men came up with spades and started the exhumation. Only a thin layer covered the bodies. The first body that was taken out was that of a woman clutching a baby in her arms. All the time the wailing and crying of the Jews could be heard. Some of them threw themselves to the ground in pain. Nina and I could not bear to watch.

The opening of the mass grave continued. Nina stayed at home. I had to go again because they wanted me to identify the bodies. From behind the castle, they took out 19 people from a single grave. Among them was young Ohl, his wife, their beautiful daughter Naomi, who I had held so often in my arms and on my knees. Apart from them, I was also forced to identify in this grave, many friends, now in their new role as dead men. Every last one of them, children and all, had been shot in the head. Only one of the victims has his skull crushed. Witnesses had told how the victims had dug graves for themselves, and then after that they had stood by the graves and been shot to death. A child had been pushed into the grave in tears. A farmer who was forced to cover the grave had heard the child's cries for a long time after he had been covered with earth. This testimony had been entered into the protocol. In the forest next to Lubyanki, they found a mass grave with 72 prisoners, victims of the first action. This was also opened up in the presence of the investigating committee. These victims had been killed by minor officers who had shouted "Forward to dig your graves!" They gave the victims spades and forced them to do their dirty work. And while the Jews, confused and frightened, were digging their graves with the full knowledge that they were shortly to enter them, the hangmen, true to their infamous fashion, started to prepare their machine gun. The Jews were then stood by the grave and the machine gun passed along the line of victims. They all fell tidily arranged. Only the privileged were given the special mingling with the dust and their shouts only ending as their souls gave up. These first victims of the mass murders were still dressed when they were shot. The ones that came later were forced to undress before they were annihilated. The junior officers always made certain that the clothes were tidily arranged. Only the privileged were given the special task of murderers and the commando recruits were specially trained in how to fire.

After the terrible times that had befallen the population, Zbaraz returned to peace time. The summer harvest was brought to market. There were plenty of fruit and vegetables. An old woman stood in the middle of the market with a large tray. Wordlessly, she offered homemade cakes. She had white hair and her stare seemed to go on forever. This was a woman from Tarnopol, and it was amazing that she had stayed alive. She had come from a good house. All her relations were buried in a mass grave.

During the initial period after we had been saved, we were under the wing of the Red Army. Now started a daily battle to find bread. I tried to make myself useful, working now here and now there. Many families gave us work and assistance. But the town of Zbaraz remained a very strange place for us, a place that was a mixture of redemption and the most terrible suffering.

On the 7th of November the Russians celebrated their revolution. We Jews that remained celebrated this day in the synagogue in the form of a Thanksgiving. There were no more than two dozen of us survivors that gathered here. With great sorrow, we remembered the wretched victims. We thanked God for saving us. Among the remains of the synagogue, I found torn burnt fragments of the torah scrolls.

With the consent of the others, I took these burned pages with me to accompany me wherever I go. With death ravaging Europe, I wanted these pages accompanying me and to serve as a terrible warning to the world to remind the world of the deeds, performed by the lowest of me.

One day the church bells of Zbaraz rang. The observant crossed themselves and the Russians lowered their flags. The market place was festive, Germany had surrendered. The war was over.

Hate is a difficult word. Hate, madness, and fanaticism bring catastrophe. I don't hate anyone. I don't even hate people. I suffered greatly from the Nazi rule, but I would not dare to act as judge on them. It is wrong to forgive. I cannot free the accused of their guilt, but man is unable to pass justice on such deeds. God alone can judge them for the inhumane way that they behaved towards their fellow humans. He alone has the power to be merciful, where man is unable to feel mercy.

INDEX

Please note that the index on the following pages *does not include names in the lists on page 72, 96 and 101*, so please review those lists separately when looking for specific people.

www.ingramcontent.com/pod-product-compliance
Lightning Source LLC
Chambersburg PA
CBHW050414110426
42812CB00006BA/1884